D1565167

DUCK AND COVER

DUCK AND COVER

A NUCLEAR FAMILY

KATHIE FARNELL

THE UNIVERSITY OF SOUTH CAROLINA PRESS

© 2017 University of South Carolina

Published by the University of South Carolina Press
Columbia, South Carolina 29208

www.sc.edu/uscpress

Manufactured in the United States of America

25 24 23 22 21 20 19 18 17
10 9 8 7 6 5 4 3 2 1

Library of Congress Cataloging-in-Publication Data
Names: Farnell, Kathie.
Title: Duck and cover : a nuclear family / Kathie Farnell.
Description: Columbia, South Carolina : University of
South Carolina Press, [2017]
Identifiers: LCCN 2016058016 | ISBN 9781611177602 (hardcover : alk. paper)
Subjects: LCSH: Farnell, Kathie—Childhood and youth. |
Girls—Alabama—Montgomery—Biography. | Children—United States—Social
life and customs—20th century. | Whites—Alabama—Montgomery—Social life
and customs—20th century. | Montgomery (Ala.)—Social life and
customs—20th century. | Montgomery (Ala.)—Biography.
Classification: LCC F334.M753 F37 2017 | DDC 976.1/47—dc23
LC record available at https://lccn.loc.gov/2016058016

This book was printed on recycled paper with
30 percent postconsumer waste content.

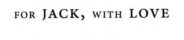

FOR JACK, WITH LOVE

CONTENTS

ACKNOWLEDGMENTS

Thanks to the members of Donna Esslinger's memoir class for getting me started, especially to Jan Pruitt and Carol Anne Brown. Other enthusiastic early readers include Steve Rathe, Dr. Glen Bannister, and Dr. Norman MacMillan.

Especial thanks to everyone at University of South Carolina Press, most of all to Linda Fogle.

My highest thanks to Jack, for everything.

If you think I'm going to thank the kid who brought the skeleton to school, you can forget it.

FALLOUT

It was the first day of school, and it was hot.

Sure it was September, but 1958 had been a hot year. I was wishing I could have worn shorts. Instead, I had on a plaid dress with a scratchy collar, which I tugged as I posed for my photo. If I had been able to read, I would have known the big sign behind me said "Cloverdale School, Montgomery, Alabama."

If I had been able to read, I would not have been in this situation.

"Quit it!" my father yelled. "Quit yanking your collar! Smile!" I managed an insincere smile. "Bigger! Smile bigger!" My father was having some trouble with the camera. He had lost his right arm in a hunting accident when he was a teenager—I usually told people he had lost it fighting the Nazis—and my mother ordinarily took the photos, but he had snatched the camera away from her. It was just as well; she was having trouble handling both their briefcases while trying to keep her hat from blowing off. They were on the way to their law office, which is why they had dropped me off at school so early that the door was still locked.

Being first into the classroom got me a prime seat near the wide-open window, through which a hot breeze wafted. Luckily, there was a fan swiveling across the front of the room, and by leaning one way or the other I could manage to stay in front of it.

By lunchtime I was getting seasick.

The lunchroom didn't do anything for my equilibrium; it smelled sort of like dishwater mixed with Lysol. However, it had two fans, so at least I felt a little cooler as I shouldered my way through the mob of kids and got handed a plastic tray piled with assorted stuff. Once I sat down and looked at the food, I perked up a little.

Turnip greens!

These greens were topped with black things that looked like chunks of hard-boiled egg, except for being black, but at least they were something I recognized. I poked the kid next to me: "Not bad, huh?"

She just looked at me.

I speared a hearty forkful, bit down, and spit the greens into my paper napkin. Black eggs aside, they tasted like they had been boiled in a tin can for two or three days. I was horrified. "There's something wrong with the turnips!" I blurted. The kid gave me another look. "Them ain't turnips," she said. "Them is spinach." I stared at my plate in disbelief. "They ain't!" I said. I knew about spinach from television, and there was no way Popeye was going to eat something like this.

Not even noon on the first day of school, and it was official: I was in over my head.

When they came back from the drugstore, my First Day of School photos were blurred except for one which clearly showed me looking apprehensive. The pixie haircut wasn't helping. I didn't know if the intent had been to make me look like Tinkerbell, but anybody could have foreseen that it wouldn't work. Tinkerbell had blonde curls, while my hair was straight, brown, and, following the haircut, practically nonexistent.

The haircut was doubly unfortunate since I had been expected to score some sort of social success at school. "You'll meet a lot of nice children," my mother had beamed. At Morningview Baptist Church, the other kids were less optimistic. "Cloverdale," said Lorraine Key darkly. "That's the snob school."

So far, nothing snobbish had occurred, unless spinach was considered a snob vegetable, but I was on the alert nevertheless.

Even my little brothers Ray and Clay noticed that the school year wasn't the unqualified success that I had predicted. Ray was four, Clay a year younger, and both were enrolled in Gantt's Kindergarten, which in retrospect was looking better and better. Each morning I watched with something approaching envy as they toddled off to Gantt's marshaled by Libby, who had worked for us since before I was born and whose current assignment consisted largely of dragging Ray and Clay out of the street. Granny, the other member of our household, had nearly three years' formal schooling under her belt but had retained little from her academic career except the ability to write her name and a stockpile of nineteenth-century playground insults, of which "Go to Halifax" was the most impressive.

As the school year progressed, lunchtime continued to cause me unease, especially since I couldn't identify much of the food. Right before Thanksgiving, I rejected a hunk of boiled cauliflower because I thought it was something's brain. My misapprehension was not all that far-fetched, considering that earlier in the week a kid named Tommy Turner had brought a human skeleton for show-and-tell. The thing, which he claimed was from his grandfather's medical office, sat hunched up in a cylindrical carrying case with a flat top, possibly designed to be used as extra seating. Our teacher, Mrs. Willet, was a gray-haired, formidable lady who probably remembered Appomattox. When somebody asked who the skeleton used to be, she waved her hand dismissively: "Probably some convict." For the rest of the year, I couldn't look at the front of the room for fear the thing might suddenly have rematerialized there.

You could say there was something in the air. Around our house, things had been rather tense since the Montgomery bus boycott, during which my father had accused Libby of being in league with the Communists. It was possible that he was just annoyed at having to pick Libby up every morning, but the incident still worried me. Besides Libby, the only Communist I knew was Nikita Khrushchev, whom I had confused with the devil. Everybody seemed worried. The newspapers were full of ads for fallout shelters. The shelters looked nice—one of them had a ping-pong table—but they cost two thousand dollars, so obviously we weren't going to get one. It's possible that my family, and in fact my entire neighborhood, didn't fully grasp the situation, because when the air-raid siren accidentally went off in the middle of the night, every house on the block switched on its lights, and we all ran out into the street, looking up.

The public-school system determined to fill the information gap. The whole first grade was issued comic books about fallout. These books featured nicely dressed children who were minding their own business when the air-raid siren sounded. Displaying remarkable self-possession, the kids squirted the hose on the roof—nobody ever explained why, but I suppose water diluted the fallout—and then went into their two-thousand-dollar fallout shelter to listen to the short-wave radio, which we also didn't have.

The comic book was honest about what your chances were if you didn't have a shelter or a hose. "Fallout can even come through glass!" The book indicated that you could make a last-ditch effort at survival by crawling under a bed, but I'd given up.

That's it, I thought. This stuff can come through glass.

Mrs. Willet also had read the comic. A directive came from the principal that we should participate in fallout drills, an activity which involved crouching under our flimsy plywood desks. Mrs. Willet was not having any. We, she announced, were not going to die hiding under any desk. "We are going to die sitting up straight!"

That's telling them, I thought, glancing defiantly at the windows.

LIBBY

Libby's real name was Olivia Love. She was brown rather than black, had high cheekbones, and referred to the color of her hair as "jet." It looked black to me. She was the same age as my mother, and weighed 140 pounds. I knew because I had asked her. Libby lived in a neighborhood called Chicken Shack, right off the Mobile Road, and rode the bus to our house every day except Sunday.

During the bus boycott, which I dimly remembered, my father had gotten mad at Libby for refusing to ride the bus. "You scared of some old Abernathy!" said my father. "I don't know no old Abernathy!" said Libby. I wondered what an Abernathy was. It sounded Irish.

We always ran to meet Libby when she got off the bus, but the glee was largely one-sided. Even though the boycott was over, Libby was a dissatisfied employee.

She complained pretty frequently about me and my brothers, specifically our habit of tormenting her with an incredibly real-looking rubber snake that Ray had brought in from somewhere. The usual scenario involved planting the snake in a kitchen drawer or somewhere

4

else Libby was sure to look. Libby would yank the drawer open, jump, and yell "Whoa shit!"— at which we would threaten to tell our parents that she had said *shit*. "I said 'shoot!'" Libby would maintain. It was our word against hers, so we had to give up at this point. The phony snake always put Libby in a very bad mood. "Treat me worsen a dog," she would say. Snakes aside, her main complaint seemed to be that we took her for granted. "Don't pay no attention to me whatsoever," she would say. "Act like I ain't even here."

She also objected to my grandmother, who didn't interact much with Libby other than by uttering "Hmpf" or "Pshaw" whenever she saw her. The problem, according to Libby, was Granny's entire attitude. "I hope I ain't here when old Miss Farnell die," she would remark. "Because the devil coming for her in person." Once Libby became so irritated with Granny that she officially quit. She was gone for two days, during which time my father yelled at Granny nearly nonstop.

Libby coped with job dissatisfaction by establishing a routine. As soon as she got to our house, she would go in the utility room back of the garage and change into a gray uniform and shoes which had the sides cut out in order, she said, "to fit her foots." Although Libby's main job seemed to be entertaining me and my brothers, occasionally she would take a stab at cleaning the house. This was a thankless task.

Our house was made of brick and looked nice from the street, even though it no longer had the big awning with an F on it which I had seen in an old photo. The house had been built in 1920 by a doctor who had promptly, according to the story, gone into the dining room and shot himself. This was a shame since the dining room, despite its history of violence, was almost as nice as the living room. They both had chandeliers; the living room also had a marble fireplace. Once you got past those rooms, things went downhill. We had six people living in a house with three bedrooms and one bathroom, so the place stayed in a certain amount of disarray. Then there was the floor furnace which, with the gas logs, was the source of heat for the house. My brother Ray's official hobby was spitting in the furnace, which was located right in the doorway to the living room, making it dangerous to pass that way during cold weather. In winter, we kept a pot of water boiling away on the furnace to humidify the air. This pot, although an additional hazard, came in handy whenever Ray caused a fire with his secondary hobby, throwing crayons down into the furnace.

If Libby decided to try cleaning the house, she would usually just drag the Hoover out and roll over the living-room rug, pausing occasionally to catch up on whatever we were watching on television.

When the weather was nice, we would walk with Libby down to the traffic light which we called the Red Light, since it was never green. When we crossed the street, Libby would urge us to run. "You're not supposed to run across the street," I would say, to which Libby would respond, "If you don't run, you get mashed flatter than a cheese."

As we walked, Libby would fill us in on the odder aspects of life in her neighborhood. "There a man down there, he shell-shock," she would say. "He walk around with no clothes on. There a lady, she got false teeth. She hang 'em on a string around her neck." Libby's grandmother, who lived in a little tumble-down house farther out in the country, came in for her fair share of excitement. "My grandmama, one time she got a hog. He eat so much till he bust open."

This was pretty alarming, especially since I occasionally went to Libby's grandmother's house to visit my chicken. I didn't remember ever taking ownership of this particular chicken, but at some point I had been told that I had a chicken that was living with Libby's grandmother, so, when we went by there, I always stopped to say hello. Libby's grandmother also had a hog. I couldn't tell how much he had been eating, so I stayed away from him.

After I started school, my time with Libby was somewhat limited, though she would walk down to the school with Ray and Clay to collect me at three o'clock, and I still saw her on Saturdays.

Whatever else we lacked, my brothers and I were an ideal audience for Libby's impersonations. If things got dull, she would summarize episodes of *Stella Dallas,* a radio series she followed. She always acted out all the parts while narrating. "Stella Dallas, she hide and see her boyfriend with this other lady. So Bam! She shoot him and then, Bam! She shoot her too." Libby clutched her chest, reeling around.

"What happened then, Libby?"

Libby would straighten up, looking exasperated. "Then the Police come. What you think happen?"

Despite Libby's gift for drama, her favorite role was a comic one, based on the episode of *I Love Lucy* in which Lucy tries to make a television commercial and accidentally gets drunk on the sponsor's tonic.

"Old Lucy get drunk," Libby would announce, rising to her feet. She would hold up an imaginary bottle, take a swig, bat her eyes and say "Taste just like candy!!!" while we rolled around on the ground laughing.

As far as I was concerned, Libby was a permanent feature, but one Saturday she announced this wasn't the case. She would not be around forever. She was not just making this statement in response to the latest snake episode. The wheels were in motion. When her grandmother died, she was going to move up north. "Oh," I said, figuring it was no use to ask when her grandmother planned to die, or whether I could just go ahead and get the chicken.

We were having this conversation in the backyard, close to the hedge. Suddenly I noticed a green snake slithering along the fence, headed straight for Libby. "Snake!" I yelled. Libby had not been rendered cynical by her encounters with fake snakes. She obligingly jumped, then, seeing an actual snake, said "Huh."

"I saved your life," I said complacently.

"That. A. Garter. Snake," gritted Libby.

"It's still a snake," I said.

The debate was cut short by Clay, who made a gasping noise. Apparently seeing the snake had caused him to swallow a piece of ice the wrong way. He was prone to do this; once in Morrison's Cafeteria, he had started turning blue and a waiter had had to hit him on the back. He was turning blue now. Libby slammed him on the back. The ice flew out.

Clay recovered his color. "Thank you, Libby," he said solemnly.

Libby smiled. "You welcome."

CHRISTMAS

You could tell it was Christmas in our neighborhood. Harry Falk, standing in his front yard under a big sign that said Peace on Earth, was throwing rocks at Maureen Clements. On the other side of the street, the teenager Celia Bronson, wearing a tight red and green sweater and black toreador pants, was standing in her parents' driveway, smoking a cigarette and ignoring the small boy, invariably introduced as "Celia's little brother," who clung to her ankle. Patty Harris's front window had sprouted its usual aluminum tree. At least once before Christmas, we would see Patty's mother chasing her out of the house with a belt.

Our Christmases usually followed a routine. Right after Thanksgiving, we would pick out a tree. I always wanted a pink one, and my mother always vetoed the idea on grounds of tackiness. We decorated the tree with glass balls my father had gotten during World War II (the box showed Uncle Sam shaking hands with Santa Claus) and other ornaments from the boxes that Libby had labeled "Shinny Beeds. Babby Jesus." Once we got the ornaments on the tree, we threw tinsel at it.

On Christmas Eve or Christmas Day, depending on when they could catch a ride, Libby and anybody else who worked for us would show up at the door and announce "Christmas Gift!" meaning that they wanted a Christmas gift. We were always absolutely delighted to see them, although they left right after getting their presents. Granny took a dim view of the whole transaction. "Ain't none of them give me nothing," she would point out.

Granny, in fact, usually spent holidays in a state my mother referred to as "getting up on her high horse." One year my father got so irritated at Granny's attitude that he took back all the presents he had bought her and got a refund.

The following December, my father announced that we would go to Mississippi for Christmas to visit my mother's Aunt Katherine. Granny, he continued, eyeing Granny narrowly, would spend Christmas with Mrs. Pilson, who lived in a big haunted-looking house down the street.

Mama had lived with Aunt Katherine when she was little, and Aunt Katherine was as close as I got to a grandmother, if you didn't count Granny. It was a long way to Mississippi, so we left early one morning. Since we didn't have a heater in the car, we threw in a bunch of quilts and got under them. When we reached the town of Laurel, Mississippi, we turned off the highway into a confusing maze of little dirt roads. My mother began cautioning us about how to behave. For one thing, we weren't supposed to run around without shoes. I doubted there was much chance of that, since it was December. Mama was apparently still upset about our visit last July. Seeing us barefooted, Aunt Katherine had said in a jolly voice, "Well, it's obvious they come of good pioneer stock." This sounded like a compliment, but my mother had looked at the floor and then told us to put our shoes on.

The best thing about visiting Aunt Katherine was the fact that she had a lot of chickens. The second best thing was that my father never yelled, much less hit anybody, around Aunt Katherine. However, usually the minute we left he would start up again. Both my parents got quiet as we drove through the pine thickets.

Finally we burst into a sort of clearing, and there was the town of Ovett, where my great-grandfather had once owned a sawmill; now all that was left of the town were twenty or thirty houses around a crossroads.

Aunt Katherine lived in a big white house with a sagging porch which she shared with her brother, Uncle Jule. Neither one of them had ever been married, though, according to my mother, some doctor had made Aunt Katherine several good offers. Uncle Jule was thin, gray, and vague; he smelled like some sort of medicine and his eyes were always bloodshot. Aunt Katherine was round and looked a lot like I envisioned Mrs. Santa Claus. She had been a school principal and now she supported herself partly by giving piano lessons; there was a piano against one wall, topped with the china flamingo I had gotten her the last time we went to Gulf Shores. Against another wall was the television set my mother had sent her from Sears. On a third wall next to the fireplace was a tall shelf of books left over from Aunt Katherine's father, who had once had some money. The fireplace itself was the only source of heat in the room; as we came in we found it

9

roaring and Uncle Jule poking it with a broom handle. The linoleum, which had a pattern of roses, creaked. Overhead, a single light bulb with a pull chain dangled from the ceiling, throwing weird shadows on the walls.

I immediately ran out to see the chickens, who lived in and around a little shed. Some of Aunt Katherine's cats collected at the wire fence to watch the chickens and me. When I finished talking to the chickens I went back in the house where Mama was putting our suitcases in the room which had been hers. It still had a row of perfume atomizers lined up on the dressing table. The heat from the fireplace didn't get all the way back to the bedroom. When it was time to go to bed, I crawled under the pile of quilts. It felt like the sheets had been hung up outside for a couple of days so I rolled up in a ball with my head under the covers.

At some point in the middle of the night I was awakened by a tremendous bang. I thought something had exploded, but it turned out to be Uncle Jule, shooting a possum that had gotten in the henhouse. By the time I got out of bed, he had the dead possum stretched out on the back porch. It was gray, and looked like a rat except for being about four feet long. I could see its teeth. I went back to bed but kept seeing those teeth every time I closed my eyes.

The next day I was supposed to go with Uncle Jule to cut down a Christmas tree. We walked past the chickens and the outhouse, which hadn't been used since Mama had paid to have a bathroom tacked onto the back of the house. At this point, I got into trouble.

There were cockleburs everywhere, and they kept getting on me. I had on mittens, which made it worse. If I tried to get the burrs off me or out of my hair, all I did was transfer them to my mittens. They were also getting on my socks.

"Stop!" I said to Uncle Jule, who had gotten a considerable way in front of me. "I'm in the burrs."

Uncle Jule pointed down a faint dirt track which led into the woods. All I could see was more cockleburs. "The trees're down here," he said.

I'd had enough. "I'm going back to the house," I said. I was a little disappointed when he showed up back at the house about thirty minutes later, dragging a big cedar tree. Later that day, Aunt Katherine announced that we would make ornaments for the tree. First we strung popcorn. My mother and Aunt Katherine cut red and green construction paper into strips and Ray and Clay glued them together into chains. We put glue on Styrofoam balls, bells, and stars, then sprinkled gold glitter on them. My father and Uncle Jule had disappeared in the direction of the back porch. Once in a while, I could hear glass clinking out there. When we got the ornaments on it, the tree looked almost as good as our tree in Montgomery except for not having any tinsel.

After supper, Aunt Katherine said we would sing Christmas carols. She sat down at the piano. We were in the middle of "Silent Night" when we heard it—a long, quavering moan from outside, somewhere up in the air. The moan rose to a whistle, then subsided into something that sounded almost like a horse neighing, except for being in the air. "What's that?' I asked. My mother and father looked at each other uncomfortably. "Screech owl," said my mother nervously. I swallowed hard. Granny had told me several times about somebody named Old Man Routmore, who had died two days after he heard the screech owl. Aunt Katherine shrugged. "Just a superstition," she said. "It's right over the house," said my father, pointing unsteadily to the ceiling.

Uncle Jule, whose eyes were more bloodshot than usual, hiccuped. The moaning sound rose again, a sound like something crying up in a tree. Ray and Clay started whimpering. "Oh, go on and chase it away, then," said Aunt Katherine.

Uncle Jule poked the fire vigorously, nearly falling into it. A stream of sparks roared up the chimney. He hobbled over to the door, yanked it open and stuck his head out. "Git!" he yelled. The moaning noise stopped.

After that, we sang a little more, but our hearts weren't in it, so we went to bed. The next morning, we opened our presents. I got modeling clay and a little fur hat. Ray and Clay got bird whistles, which made a warbling sound, and bedroom slippers with an Indian on them.

We had pancakes for breakfast; then it was time to drive home so we could open our own Christmas presents. I hugged Aunt Katherine. "Don't you want to stay with me?" she asked. "You could learn to play the piano. You could help us feed the chickens." I thought it over. I was already learning piano, and didn't like it, but the chickens were a draw. "Okay," I said. Everybody laughed. I realized she hadn't been serious. "I guess I should go to Montgomery," I said.

We all got in the car. I was in the back seat with Ray and Clay, both of whom were blowing their bird whistles. "Stop that noise," said my father shortly. "I don't know what she could have been thinking," said my mother, holding her head.

I wished they would stop, too. The bird whistles quavered, like something crying.

EASTER EGG

There was going to be an Easter egg hunt at school for the first grade. I was absent the day they made the announcement, so I heard about it from Sarah Stein. Sarah and I had gotten to be friends, since her parents owned Stein's Art Supply and she had a five-dollar box of Crayola crayons.

"Can I borrow your Orchid?" I asked. We were coloring a scene from *The Cat in the Hat,* and my fifteen-cent box of crayons didn't even have Pink.

"Really. Easter egg hunt," repeated Sarah. "All sorts of prizes and there's going to be a gold egg."

"Right," I said doubtfully.

"You know," added Sarah casually, "at my house we celebrate Passover right before Easter." This was typical Sarah. She had to make sure everybody knew that her family got to celebrate about thirty extra holidays per year. Roughly ten minutes after I met her, she had announced that, in addition to Christmas, Easter, Thanksgiving, and the Fourth of July, red-letter days at the Stein house included Purim, Hanukkah, Yom Kippur, Rosh Hashanah, and Sukkot, which, according to Sarah, was the most fun since you got to sit in a hut.

"Right," I had said. I wasn't sure I believed her about some of these holidays.

Though I regretted not having the opportunity to sit in a hut, I was very enthusiastic about Easter and felt sure that my egg-finding skills would make me the envy of the entire class. My family had had mixed luck when it came to Easter. As a kid in Pike County, Alabama, my father had specialized in using a guinea-hen egg, which evidently had a shell the consistency of cement, to break all the other kids' eggs. In Ovett, where my mother grew up, the emphasis was on consumption; she had once eaten two dozen Easter eggs. Though it had seemed like a good idea at the time, the experience had given her a phobia. Now she wouldn't eat eggs under any circumstances.

I talked a lot about the Easter egg hunt since it made my brothers envious—especially the part about the gold egg—and distracted my father from nagging me about my grades. First grade wasn't exactly the academic big time, but for some reason my father had decided that I should triumph over all the other kids in every subject, especially spelling. He had gone to a one-room school at which, he claimed, the teacher was even more ignorant than the students. My mother had had rather the opposite experience since Aunt Katherine had been a school principal.

When I washed out of the spelling bee by leaving the second *p* out of *pumpkin,* it was a major blow, especially since the whole debacle came just ten days after Aunt Katherine's funeral.

By the morning of the egg hunt, I needed something to restore my self-image. As we trooped out to the playground, swinging our baskets, my spirits rose. I was looking forward to hauling in those eggs. The hunt was being overseen by the shop teacher, Miss Mickey Cain, who was the size of a tank, wore a dress that appeared to have been made out of sweatshirt material, and went around all day emitting blasts on the stainless-steel whistle she wore around her neck. Miss Cain was always in a bad mood, probably because teaching had not been her first career choice. According to rumor, she had once been a lady wrestler who had lost her job for killing her opponent.

"On yer marks!" bellowed Miss Cain. We got on our marks.

"Go!" She followed up this announcement with a piercing blast on the whistle, and this was where I got into trouble. Whenever I heard a loud noise, it was my reaction to drop to the ground, covering my head with both arms. I didn't do it intentionally and was always as surprised as anybody. This automatic response had saved my bacon a number of times in dealing with my father, but unfortunately the reaction wasn't limited to hearing him yell—any sudden loud noise, even if it was coming from *Gunsmoke,* was liable to set it off.

"Get up! Get up!" Sarah Stein urged. "This is no time to fall down! Come on!" She ran off toward a likely-looking tree and yanked a purple egg out of a crook in one of its limbs.

I staggered to my feet. Where was I supposed to look? There was a patch of weeds—too late. Maureen Clements was already grabbing a yellow egg from it.

Well, what about the retaining wall?

"TWEEEET!"

By the time I got up and dusted myself off, Becca Hollis was digging a red egg from behind the wall, and Miss Cain was hauling Harry Falk, who had been throwing eggs, off the premises by his ear. "Come on!"—Sarah again. "Look!" she added proudly, indicating her basket. Gold egg. "You don't have any eggs yet? You've really got to start looking. Here, you can have one of mine." She plopped a blue egg into my basket and barreled off toward the flagpole, yelling "I saw it first!"

Warily, I glanced around. No Cain; just a jumbled mass of kids crawling through bushes, peering into culverts, shoving each other out of the way, and hurling the occasional egg. Surely there must be someplace else to look.

The barbecue pit! Off to one side of the playground, the school maintained a ten-foot-long barbecue pit. Plenty of good hiding places. I ran toward it.

"TWEEEET!"

Blearily, I sat up. Miss Cain was hollering "Hunt's over! Hunt's over! Drop that egg!" This was directed at Maureen Clements, who was taking aim.

"Students," our teacher Mrs. Willet was beaming. "We have a winner for the gold egg." Sarah waved graciously. "Here is your prize, Sarah." Mrs. Willet reached into a cardboard box at her feet and hauled out an enormous chocolate Easter rabbit, handing it to Sarah, who grinned broadly.

"And—the prize for the most eggs," she brought out a slightly smaller rabbit and handed it to the cutthroat Maureen Clements, who looked smug.

14

"Now, we have a consolation prize"—this was a rabbit which looked every bit as big as the one Maureen was now eating—"for the student who did not find any eggs. Anyone? Anyone?"

Nobody said anything.

"Well, then, we have a runner-up for most eggs." She handed the rabbit to Tommy Turner. I could dimly hear Harry Falk saying it was a gyp and if he'd known there was going to be a runner-up he wouldn't have thrown all those eggs.

I looked down. There, rolling around in my basket, was the solitary blue egg, mocking me.

Thanks a lot, Sarah.

HULA HOOP NATION

Every morning in first grade, all the girls would line their hula hoops up against the wall. They made quite a pile. I had a light green hoop which compared favorably with the others, although Sarah Stein had a gold one.

I didn't see anything odd about twenty girls trundling large plastic hoops into a classroom, and apparently neither did Mrs. Willet. The school had already fought and lost the hula hoop battle, though it was still holding the line on gum.

When the bell rang for recess, we ran to grab our hoops. This led to some confusion if one's hoop was at the bottom of the stack. We spilled out onto the playground, which was a big patch of dirt centered around one large sycamore tree, and immediately began slinging our hoops. The usual strategy in hula hooping was to see how many you could sling around your midsection at one time. I could do ten on a good day. Nobody, not even Sarah Stein, owned more than one regular-sized hoop, so you had to borrow other people's. This frequently led to altercations. In addition to the big hoops, there were small hoops for arms, ankles, or neck. These hoops struck me as a waste of money, since it was perfectly possible to sling a regular-sized hoop around your limb of choice, though it would sort of hurt your neck.

We never got tired of hooping. For one thing, hoops were versatile. If you got bored with slinging one around your waist, you could use it as a jump rope. You could also throw it like a boomerang, though it usually wouldn't come back, in which case you had to chase it.

When the hoops came out in earnest, we knew it was spring. Hula hoops were a warm-weather activity; you couldn't sling a hoop while wearing a coat. During the winter we lugged the hoops around anyway but couldn't do much with them. Once in a while somebody would try hooping in a house, but it always ended badly.

My father said that hula hoops were a fad and that the fad would blow over. He also said hoops were nothing new; when he was little, girls used to play with barrel hoops by rolling them along the ground, hitting them with sticks. This didn't work all that well with hula hoops.

As the weather got warmer, hoops were everywhere. If you invited a kid over to play, you were also inviting her hoop. This was particularly true in the case of Patty Harris. Her mother had bought her a black hoop made out of galvanized rubber or something. It weighed about ten pounds, and when she tried to sling it, she fell down.

One day in late spring, there was an announcement. There was going to be a hula hoop contest at school. This on its face seemed unbelievable, but it turned out that the contest would be held during something called Play Day. Play Day, which fell close to the last day of school, was a dying tradition at Cloverdale. We were told solemnly that this would probably be the last Play Day, because there were too many of us. I didn't see how this was our fault. On Play Day, students were allowed to come to school in shorts, which meant that you were a lot cooler while you were in the building, and then, to top things off, you spent most of the day outside, playing.

I wondered what Alice Cook was going to do. Alice didn't have a hoop. Her parents were missionaries, and according to the book *Pollyanna*, all missionaries got their clothes from barrels that well-meaning people had sent to the Congo or wherever they were. By the time Alice lined up for her clothes, they must have gotten close to the bottom of the barrel. She always wore long sleeves, skirts which would have been stylish had we been living in the year 1900, and knee socks.

I figured that for Play Day, she would just stay home, or else show up in bloomers.

Alice showed more fight than I would have expected, though, because when Play Day rolled around she appeared in knee-length pants which, while not exactly shorts, weren't exactly anything else, and she had on no socks whatsoever. Immediately after the Pledge of Allegiance, she joined the rest of us as we trooped out to the playground. It wasn't just the first graders; all the elementary grades were having contests, and all the contestants were girls. The boys, who had studiously ignored hula hooping, stood around in a sullen mob at the edge of the playground.

I was having a good day and managed to sling twelve hoops at once. Not a record, but not bad. Sarah Stein, whose gold hoop was earning her some envious glances, was going for spectacle. She borrowed everyone's hoops, slung them around her waist, then added small hoops around her neck and arms. Obviously, this wasn't going to end well, so I moved in for a closer look. Sarah spun valiantly for a while, fourteen or fifteen hoops orbiting her, but then she stumbled, and the hoop around her neck flew off, straight toward the herd of boys. It hit Harry Falk, the meanest boy in school, who had once tried to kill Dickie Pate by locking him in a shed and spraying Raid through a crack.

"Hey!" yelled Harry. He picked up the hoop and hurled it straight at Maureen Clements, the meanest girl in school, who had once shoved her brother off a garage.

"Oh yeah?" Unhesitatingly, Maureen grabbed a hoop off Sarah (which was fairly easy, since Sarah had now fallen down and was just lying there under a pile of hoops), swung, and connected with Harry's nose. If she had only had Patty Harris's industrial-strength hoop, she would have killed him. Just my luck, I thought, that Patty goes to Catholic school.

The boys had been uncharacteristically slow to pick up on hula hoops' potential as weaponry, but they could take a hint. There was a general rush after hoops. Some of the kids from the older grades were using them as lassos, throwing them around the necks of fleeing kids. I picked up my hoop and followed Sarah, who was evidently worried that her gold hoop would fall victim to looters, around the side of the building. Over the yelling, we could hear Miss Cain blowing her whistle. "That's it!" she bellowed. "No more Play Day!"

Sarah shook her head. "No more Play Day," she said.

"Yeah," I said.

The problem, as I saw it, went clear beyond Play Day. Hoops were a lot of trouble.

What were we going to do with them in the summer? You couldn't carry them on a bike. I'd tried. What would we do with them at the beach? You could still sling your hoop, but that was it; no rolling them around with all that sand. Also, how would they fit in the car?

I sighed. Maybe hula hoops were a fad. Just then, I spotted Alice Cook under the sycamore tree. She was watching a kid doing something. This kid was concentrating hard, swinging his arm out and jerking his hand up and down, completely oblivious to the battle of the hula hoops. What was he doing? I got a little closer.

He had a yo-yo.

A purple yo-yo.

I dropped my hoop.

GRANNY

Granny insisted on keeping a chamber pot under her bed. Every morning, the first thing Libby had to do was empty the pot. This put her in a bad mood right off the bat. Granny, meanwhile, would have already gotten up, put on a cotton dress, cotton stockings and a cotton apron, and gone out in the yard to get a twig which she used to brush her teeth. Later in the day, she would use another twig to dip snuff from a little can she kept in the top drawer of her dresser. I was fascinated by the snuff, which I erroneously assumed would taste like Nestle's Quik.

After she got her snuff, Granny would drag a hoe from the garage and start chopping weeds in the flower beds. Granny, whose official name was Armitta Farnell, was eighty years old, but she was tough and wiry. It was possible to imagine her swinging her hoe with great effect against weeds, snakes, or rival farmers. Eventually she would take a break to read the obituary column in the newspaper. My father said that, in addition to being able to read the obituaries, Granny was able to write her name, but I never saw her do it.

My father didn't get along with Granny, who was his mother. He used to say "that old woman wasn't born, she was hatched." Granny didn't get along with him, either. In fact, she didn't like my brothers, whom she once locked out of the house, or my mother—and, in that case, the feeling was mutual. Inexplicably, she liked me and expected me to tag along and watch her chop weeds.

Granny would sometimes plant flowers in the yard, but it was a thankless task because our dirt was prairie soil, which was apparently the same kind of dirt they have on the moon. In dry weather, prairie soil was hard as a brick. In rainy weather, prairie soil turned into quicksand. Granny would encourage me to grow things, but I was frustrated not only by the dirt but also by my irrational optimism in picking out seed packages for things that only grow in Mexico.

Granny seemed happiest outside, probably because it reminded her of the old days on her farm. She appeared confused by the twentieth century. Once, we were watching a television show about the Alamo. Cannons were firing, soldiers were falling off the wall, horses were running amok. Granny wandered through, surveyed the screen, snorted and left the room. It turned out that she thought we were watching the nightly news, which at the time was covering the Selma to Montgomery march.

Granny wasn't a big favorite with the neighborhood kids, most of whom she had at one time or another chased out of the yard with a broom. In fact, shortly after school ended for the summer, Harry Falk organized an anti-Granny cheer: "Today is Friday, I wish it would rain. There goes Granny, down the drain." I joined in, but I had mixed feelings. For one thing, Granny used to take me downtown with her. We went downtown the very Thursday after the anti-Granny incident.

Before we set out, Granny took off her apron and put on a somewhat better dress. She still had on cotton stockings, but she wore lace-up shoes, not the flattened-out house shoes she wore in the yard. When we got to the bus stop, the neighbors' dog, Fluffy, was also there, napping in the middle of the street. The bus pulled up short, and the driver got out, picked up Fluffy, who weighed about fifty pounds, lugged him to the curb, and got back in the bus. Then Granny and I climbed aboard. The bus, which wasn't air-conditioned and was already getting pretty hot, had a big seat that ran all the way across the back. This was obviously the best seat in the bus, since by standing on it you got a 180-degree view out the back window, but I never got to sit there except when I traveled with Libby.

Granny and I paid our ten cents each and plopped down in a front seat, just in time to avoid falling down as the bus, with a loud grinding noise, took off. The bus was usually packed; sometimes Granny even saw somebody she knew. We rolled down the street. I spotted Celia Bronson, holding her head, climb unsteadily out of a car in front of the Bronson house. She gave the bus a blank look. Celia was a puzzle. Sometimes she vanished for whole months at a time. If I happened to notice, Mama always said Celia had gone to Tuscaloosa. Maybe Celia was in college, I thought, though it seemed to be taking her a long time to graduate. I forgot all about Celia at this point, as the bus careened around a corner and I grabbed the back of the seat in front of me. Granny and I sat in silence until the bus lurched to a halt in front of H. L. Green's.

Green's was a dime store with one interesting feature—a selection of bride dolls in plastic domes. On this occasion, Granny actually bought me one. I was enchanted. I hung on to the bride doll as Granny bought some snuff and a package of sewing needles. Then we walked up the street to Morrison's Cafeteria. I kept the doll on my lap while I ate.

After lunch we walked to the beauty shop, which was located in an alley near my parents' office. Granny always had her hair done by a woman named Minnie, who had a gold tooth. By the time Granny was under the dryer, I was getting bored, even though I had my bride doll to look at. I discovered that she would close her eyes if I laid the dome on its side. At this point, I decided to call my parents' office and inform them that I had a new doll. Maybe they'd want me to drop by and demonstrate it. I got Minnie's telephone off the table where she kept the spare rollers. My father answered the phone on the first ring. "Hello!" he yelled. "Daddy," I said, "guess what?" "Don't call us down here!" he yelled, even louder. "Don't call us down here! We're just as busy as ants down here!" The phone went dead. I looked at a *Life* magazine until Granny got ready to leave.

We walked up to Rexall Drugs to wait for the bus. It was really hot by this time, so we stood under the awning. Finally, the bus pulled up and I climbed on, carefully carrying my doll. The bus route home was different from the route to town. On the homeward trip, we wound through a new part of town called Normandale. All the houses here were one-story and had picture windows and neat squares of front yard, usually without trees. Despite the heat, people were mowing the grass; the scent drifted in through the bus window. In one yard, there was a badminton net. A man hit the badminton bird over the net to two little boys who were laughing.

When we got home I put the bride doll, still in her dome, on top of the dresser in the room I shared with Granny. I didn't have any ambition of playing with my new doll, and it didn't occur to me to give her a name. As far as I knew, she was like a painting; you were just supposed to look at her.

Granny put her cotton dress back on, but she didn't go out in the yard. Instead, she headed into the dining room. Some of her bigger house plants were in there, along with a desk that my parents used when they worked at home on the weekends. It was kind of hard to get to the dining table, which was always covered with files. We ate in the kitchen.

A little later, when I was playing on the porch, Granny came and took me by the hand. She pulled me into the dining room, went over to a big Angel Wing begonia, and lifted up a leaf. There was a spray of pink flowers—the only time on record that this plant had bloomed.

Granny smiled.

VACATION

We began getting ready to go to Gulf Shores the night before. First we dragged the two suitcases out from the hall closet. My mother and father each had one, made from the same stuff used to make footballs. It doesn't seem likely that all the paraphernalia for five people could fit in two suitcases, but the only other thing I was taking was a sort of beach bag. Granny, who had her own suitcase, wasn't a light packer; she insisted on taking her wastebasket.

We usually left for the beach right after breakfast, and since we got up at five, that was pretty early.

We piled into the black Bel Air—no heater, no air-conditioner, no seatbelts. My parents got in the front with me, and everybody else climbed in the back, sitting on the floor if the seat was full. All the windows were down; my brothers and I spent the entire trip hanging our heads out the window, like dogs.

We stopped for lunch at Brewton, a town which smelled like a paper mill. Since I didn't know any better, I thought the smell had something to do with the beach. We got sandwiches from somewhere and ate near a little stream that fascinated me because the sand at its edges was full of shells. This way to the beach, I thought.

South of Stapleton, we reached the fork in the road. At this point, we usually took a left and headed straight down 59 to the beach. This time, we turned right, through Spanish Fort, on the way to pick up my half-sister Mona from the bus station in Mobile. This meant we were headed straight for the Bankhead Tunnel. As we dove into the dark, my father, as usual, pointed out that the tunnel ran under the Mobile River and that ships were passing above our heads. This was a disturbing thought; I ignored it in order to focus on holding my breath.

At the bus station, which was located in a nonpicturesque section of Mobile, we packed Mona, who was chewing gum, and her big round cardboard suitcase into the back seat. At least she hadn't brought her ukulele this time; and it was summer, so we didn't have to deal with her crinoline petticoats which would have taken up the entire car. Mona had on big sunglasses, tight blue shorts and a plaid blouse; her hair looked blonder and frizzier than it did last year. She slept most of the way to the beach. This struck me as ridiculous, especially as we reached Foley—practically within walking distance—and the atmosphere became electric. Finally we crossed the drawbridge into Gulf Shores, got our first sight of the water where the road dead-ended at the public beach, and turned left toward Ashwander's Beach Cottages, our destination. My brothers and I stuck our heads even farther out the window, trying to be first to spot the double row of red cottages perched on stilts.

At the beach, my morning routine never varied. I got up before the sun, yanked on shorts and a shirt, and ran down the front steps and the dirt drive to the beach. It was so early the white sand wasn't even white yet; it was dappled with purple and blue shadows. And it was cool. I sat down and watched the spot on the horizon where the sun eventually appeared. When my father and brothers showed up, we walked east toward Young's Cottages and the Lighthouse Motel before turning around and heading back to Ashwander's. "We walked a mile before breakfast," my father announced. My mother and Granny, who had been frying bacon and getting on each other's nerves, gave us a look. Mona, visible as a mound under a spread on the couch, pulled a pillow over her head.

Mona was not really a beach person. Once she finally got up, her whole focus lay in stuffing herself into a bikini and heading for the public beach, a place my mother didn't favor because the people there were trash. I tagged along with the idea of getting a hot dog. The trashy people at the public beach were mostly standing around smoking cigarettes. Some of the men whistled at Mona, who wagged her rear in acknowledgment. I got my hot dog and left.

It was getting hot by this time; the Gulf was a dark green striped with white foam where the waves were hitting a sandbar ten yards out.

Back at the cottage, I went looking for the Ashwanders' daughter, Evie Lynn, who was roughly my age. When we first met, I had thought her name was Evil Lynn and had said to myself, "At least she's honest." I didn't expect everything at the beach to be like it was in Montgomery—in fact, that was sort of the point—so while I wasn't too nonplussed at Evil Lynn's unusual name, I had been horrified to learn that she went to school. As far as I was concerned, this made no sense. Either you were unlucky, in which case you lived in Montgomery and went to school, or you were lucky, in which case you lived at the beach and didn't.

I was not enthusiastic about hanging around with Evie Lynn even though I had figured out that her name was really Evie, but at least she wasn't as odd as Mona. We went for a walk down the beach and came across a whole line of fish, just lying there. "Great!" I said. "Look at all these fish!" Evie Lynn agreed that it was pretty lucky, us happening across fish just there for the taking. So we picked up ten or twelve of them and took them into the motel office to her mother. Mrs. Ashwander had a very bad attitude about the whole thing, exclaiming that those fish were dead. I didn't see what the problem was; they'd be dead by the time you cooked them. I wandered back out to dump the fish on the sand. What could you expect, I thought, exasperated, from somebody who nearly named her own child Evil?

I walked out onto the rickety pier. Ashwander's pier changed from time to time, depending on how recently it had been knocked down by a storm; this version had a shady bench. I sat and looked back at the cottages. I couldn't see the public beach, which was hidden behind the Seahorse Motel, so I didn't know what Mona was doing. I could make out the heads of my father and brothers, bobbing in the water. It was odd, I thought: on the one hand, the beach did some people a world of good. I couldn't remember my father ever hitting anybody at the beach, and I probably would have noticed. On the other hand, some people didn't get anything out of it. Mona, for example, or my mother, who usually sat under a palmetto shelter reading a magazine, or especially Granny, who stayed on the screen porch of the cottage all day dipping snuff. And what about Evie Lynn, whom I spotted headed back from the cottages? Somewhere, maybe right across Highway 182 behind that stand of pine trees, lurked a school to which she'd have to return in a couple of months.

I shook my head.

BUSINESS

We should have been rich. Both my parents were lawyers. We might have been better off if my mother had gotten a job working for somebody who would pay her. She worked for my father, but he didn't give her a salary. If she wanted a Coke, she had to ask him for a nickel. My father also had trouble getting paid. He represented criminal defendants, all of whom were probably guilty and none of whom were bank robbers or anything that involved a steady income. Although my parents worked five and a half days a week, they didn't have much to show for it except a whole drawer full of murder weapons. Once when a friend of Libby's had her umbrella stolen in H. L. Green's, Libby had excitedly placed a call from the pay phone to my father, reporting the crime and demanding that my father have the offender—who apparently was notorious in the community—thrown in jail. My father explained that he was not the kind of lawyer who throws people in jail, but the kind who keeps them out. Libby didn't see any use in that, and neither did I.

My father's clients got thrown in jail pretty regularly, and my father was usually unsympathetic. Once the phone rang late one night, and a man announced frantically that he was in jail. "And you can stay there," said my father, hanging up. Robert, our yard man, got thrown in jail almost every Saturday night, and my father would get him out on Sunday, but he always insisted on waiting until after the prisoners' Sunday school, saying it wouldn't do Robert a bit of harm. Thanks to my father, Robert was fairly well versed in the Bible and was usually called on to help lead the singing.

Occasionally my parents came into some money. Once a client paid my father with a whole sack of silver dollars, probably from some long-ago train robbery, and once my father showed me his wallet, which had two one-hundred-dollar bills in it. However, the following week when I announced I needed notebook paper, my father refused to give me a dollar, saying that we were poor, and I had to settle for the twenty-five-cent package.

Part of the reason we were sometimes unexpectedly poor was my father's habit of betting on things with a group of men who hung around a shoeshine stand downtown. My father usually lost these bets, though one time he bet on the North in the Blue-Gray game and won seventy dollars. As soon as the news came over the radio, my father went excitedly to the phone and called Lobman, who was the leader of the shoeshine group. My mother was appalled. As soon as my father finished gloating and hung up, she lit into him. "What do you call yourself doing, betting against your own people?"

My father was unrepentant. "But they were going to lose," he said.

Another thing that kept us from being rich was my father's habit of loaning people money. Sometimes as a result of these loans we wound up in business. One September night, my father came home in a good mood, carrying a paper bag full of donuts. We now owned a bakery, he announced. I was amazed, even though the donuts were pretty stale. It seemed that a man had borrowed money from my father to open a bakery in Troy, about an hour south of Montgomery. When the man didn't pay him back, my father had promptly taken possession of the bakery. This, I felt, was more like it.

"We own a bakery," I said casually to Sarah Stein the next day at recess. I handed her the paper bag. "Here, have a turnover." "What?" Sarah, though clearly entranced, was skeptical. "I thought your father was a lawyer."

"He is," I said, helping myself to a donut, which had gotten kind of hard. "He's a lawyer who owns a bakery."

"Wow," said Sarah, indistinctly. "You mean," she continued, around her turnover, "he owns a bakery like Liger's?" Liger's Bakery, located in the modern Normandale Shopping Center, was Montgomery's premier destination for birthday cakes. It also had rye bread, which nobody had ever heard of, and its window featured a wedding cake topped with a plastic bride and groom.

"Uh," I said, "kind of."

Since our bakery was located in Troy, I wasn't sure about the details. Fortunately, the treats kept on coming. Every week, we'd have a bag full of donuts, cake, eclairs, pastries, cookies, and once an odd-looking braided loaf of bread—all of it somewhat the worse for wear.

Predictably, Granny was not enthused. She inspected a squashed cream puff, said "Pshaw," and after that ignored the bounty. My mother looked a little worried. "Don't they ever sell anything?" she asked.

She was the only doubter. Before long, I was the toast of recess, and Libby had gotten herself put on the prestigious Refreshments Committee at her church.

Things began going wrong shortly after Halloween. Although the treats were more numerous than ever—once including a whole perfectly good pound cake—it became obvious that our finances had taken another dive. One afternoon, I reached into the refrigerator for a jar of mayonnaise to make a sandwich. Unfortunately, I picked up the jar by its lid, which someone who wasn't me had neglected to tighten. When the jar crashed to the floor, one of the things my father screamed at me was an accusation: I had ruined a twenty-five-cent jar of mayonnaise. The following week when John Harrison, the office janitor, asked to borrow five dollars, my father didn't just yell at him and then give him the money. He threw a chair at him, yelled at him, and then gave him the money.

Finally came the official announcement. We no longer owned a bakery. I sought comfort from Libby, who was sitting mournfully under a pecan tree in the backyard. "What am I gonna do about recess?" I asked. "Recess nothing," said Libby unsympathetically. "What I'm gonna do about church?"

The next month, my father announced that we now owned a dry cleaners.

It wasn't the same.

WINTER

I hated winter. For one thing, it was at this time of year that my mother's Aunt Katherine had died. Mama and I had driven to Mississippi hoping we'd be in time, but we weren't. While we were there, it snowed three inches, an event I included in my show-and-tell report for the following week: "My aunt died, and I threw a snowball."

Winter was not only sad, it was dangerous. I had a rickrack scar running up my leg from falling on the floor furnace.

One of the worst things about winter was being cold all the time at school. At recess, I huddled in a corner, trying to pull my dress and coat down over my legs, which were freezing. Some of the girls had tights, but the trouble was they got wet really easily; one puddle and you were freezing and damp for the rest of the day.

Then one day I saw Lois Evans wearing long pants under her flimsy plaid dress. Corduroy pants. What an idea! There I was, trying to stay out of the wind by hiding behind a bush, and there she was, jumping rope.

I went straight home and told my mother. She had just come in from work, and as we talked, she took off her high heels and tied an apron over her beautiful black wool suit. In the living room, we could hear my father yelling at Ray: "You'd worry the balls off a brass monkey!" I had no idea what that expression meant, but I thought that Ray should have had enough sense to hide behind the garage when he heard the car pull up.

"Pants?" repeated my mother. She was inclined to be open-minded on the issue, maybe because she was wearing sheer nylons—her legs must have been cold, too. "I don't see why not. The school says you have to wear a dress. They didn't tell you not to wear pants too." She became thoughtful. "Aunt Katherine thought women who wore pants were common."

This was not a surprise. Aunt Katherine thought everything was common, including collards. Dinnertime at her house featured only high-class vegetables, like turnips.

Aunt Katherine or not, it was settled. The next cold day, there I was, red corduroy pants under a dress printed with little orange flowers. Since my parents left for work early, Libby was in charge of selecting my wardrobe. "I don't think this goes," I said. Libby disagreed. "That mix-match," she said firmly. "That stylish."

I may not have been stylish, but at least I was warm. As soon as the bell sounded for recess, I hurried outside. There was an array of cold-weather activities to choose from. I could throw pine cones at Tommy Turner, join a game of crack the whip under the leadership of the fiendish Maureen Clements, or play hopscotch with Becca Hollis. Or . . . what were those kids doing?

The sidewalk right outside the school door formed a fairly steep ramp. Somebody had poured a bucket of water on it. It was now an ice slide. Kids, including some girls in pants, were running, hitting the ice, trying in vain to stay upright, falling down and sliding all the way into the bushes.

The ideal activity for someone in pants. I joined the crowd. Dickie Pate was in the process of rolling off the edge of the ice. He hadn't even fallen down. He was a Yankee, which gave him an unfair advantage in anything involving extreme cold. At last it was my turn. I got a running start and launched myself down the ice. I managed to stay upright for four or five feet before falling flat and spinning off into the bushes.

I was on my third turn when the trouble started.

"Which of you hooligans is responsible for this?" It was the dreaded Miss Vinton, roughly a hundred years old with a voice like a foghorn. She stalked the halls, always carrying a yardstick which she swung like a machete. She was swinging it now. Everybody scattered. I was still trying to get myself out of the bush.

"Kathryn!" She was the only person on the planet who didn't call me Kathie. "Are you wearing Pants?"

Well, they were red, so it should have been obvious. "Yeah," I said, trying to be agreeable.

This only set her off. "Don't say 'yeah.' Say 'yes, ma'am.' Why are you wearing Pants? I always thought you were a Nice Little Girl. Nice Little Girls don't wear Pants. Do you understand me?"

"Yeah."

Despite my attempts at cordiality, it became obvious that the conversation was going nowhere, so I ran.

Around the corner of the school, some kids were singing army songs. Gary Falk, whose brother Harry was the meanest boy in school, seemed to be in charge. They were in the middle of one I already knew.

"You're in the army now. You're not behind a plow. You'll never get rich, you son of a bitch, you're in the army now." This was a pretty good song, but the details weren't clear. "Hey Gary," I said, "What's a son of a bitch?"

Gary thought it over. "It's somebody like your grandmother."

"Ah," I said.

Meanwhile, the crowd had moved on to "Popeye the Sailor Man," who, though not in the army, was included as a member of the armed services. "I'm Popeye the Sailor Man, I live in the garbage can. I eat all the turtles and spit out their girdles. I'm Popeye the Sailor Man."

Dickie Pate showed up, out of breath from outdistancing Miss Vinton. "I got a great one," he said. "My uncle said they sang this one in the war."

He took a deep breath. "Whistle while you work, Hitler is a jerk. Mussolini bit his weenie, now it doesn't squirt."

This was the most ridiculous song anybody had ever heard, easily beating Elvis Presley's "Hound Dog," so once we stopped rolling on the ground laughing, everybody happily joined in.

As I sang, I thought it over. I'd always hated winter, yet here I was, warm as toast, and having a great time. In just one morning, I had acquired the valuable skill of sliding on ice, increased my vocabulary, and learned a new song on top of it all. Winter wasn't so bad. You just had to be practical about it.

At this point, I spotted Miss Vinton barreling around the side of the building. She was swinging her yardstick.

"Son of a bitch," I said.

SPEND THE NIGHT

Becca Hollis and I had become friends in the first grade, when we found out we both knew how to swim. She had taken lessons at the Montgomery Country Club, and I had been thrown into a pond by my father. The most interesting thing about Becca was that she came from a rich family.

For a public school, Cloverdale was pretty class-conscious, and everybody knew which families were rich. Mrs. Willet had tried to level the playing field by correcting our pronunciation if we said *chimney* as *chimbley* and by asking repeatedly how many bathrooms we had at home, though what she was planning to do about it I don't know.

Becca had a big two-story house with plenty of bathrooms. Her family included older half-siblings as well as a younger brother. Her father, who had been a doctor with plenty of money, was dead. Every time I said something about Becca having a bigger house, not to mention more plumbing, than we did, my mother would say, "but her father is dead," as if you got one or the other.

Becca's mother, Mrs. Hollis, was a big, soft woman with very black hair and a booming voice. Her nickname was Priss, and she always spoke in a manner which I later recognized as ironic.

Becca's mother was undependable. One summer day when they were supposed to pick me up to go swimming at the Y, Becca and Priss had been about ninety minutes late. I stood out in front of the house for a while, then I went inside the house, then I went outside and stood in front of the house some more. There was no point in calling Becca's house because even if somebody happened to answer and you asked for Becca, the chances were that neither Becca nor the person who had originally answered would ever return to the line. It had occurred to me by the time Becca and Priss were ten minutes overdue that they were never coming and that it was liable to be dark before anybody in my house decided to come looking for me. So I started crying and when they showed up, Priss announced dramatically, "Now, see, the child's been crying," as if she had had absolutely no control over the situation despite the fact that it was her car. On the way to the pool, she ran over the curb twice, and I also noticed she was having some trouble with hiccups.

Becca used to ask me to spend the night. Usually I said no, since I was scared of spending the night, but in second grade, I was feeling braver so I said yes. Her house had a big yard; in fact, the yard went all the way through the block. Becca's yard had a chinquapin tree and, more important, a hedge in which I spotted a bird's nest. This was a lot better than my yard, which only had a swing set.

The time I spent the night, we had chicken for dinner, prepared by their black cook. It was some new sort of chicken: not fried. I went in search of the cook afterward and found her in the kitchen. "That was the best supper I ever et," I said politely. The cook, whose name was Ellen, immediately rounded upon Becca and her younger brother. "See?" she said. "This child here thank me. And she don't even live here." The situation was defused by the belated arrival of dessert— watermelon which had been frozen since last summer. "I didn't know you could freeze watermelon," I said enthusiastically, but it turned out you couldn't; it had turned to a sort of red sludge.

Entertainment after dinner included sliding down the stairs on couch cushions. I wished bitterly that I had a two-story house, though I realized that if somebody had done that at our house they would have been beaten to death; yet another instance where having a dead father sounded like it might be a good deal. Priss drank steadily from a heavy-looking glass. Once in a while she would hiccup, say "You chillen be careful!" and laugh gaily. When her glass got empty, she would call "Ellen!" and the cook would stump in, snatch the glass, stump out and bring it back filled and sloshing.

Eventually, we went to bed in Becca's room, which had two white canopy beds and its own bathroom. I didn't sleep long, and in any case at my house everybody woke up at five; eventually it became sort of light outside and I got up. Becca, from what I could see of her, was sound asleep. I wandered quietly downstairs and was surprised to find the big carved front door standing wide open. It was foggy outside. Mist drifted in the door, which I wondered if I should shut. Then I saw there was a man lying face down in the middle of the living room rug. I blinked; the man didn't seem to be dead, so I went back upstairs and pretended to be asleep until Becca woke up.

I didn't think I should mention the man, who was gone when we went downstairs. Later he turned out to be one of Becca's older half-brothers. I thought about the situation after I got home. On the one hand, I'd never seen anybody lying around our living room like they were dead. On the other hand, I'd seen nearly everything else. I was having these thoughts while sitting on the front steps. In the house, I could hear my father yelling at Clay. They were apparently in the kitchen, in the back of the house. It sounded like Clay had spilled some milk. There was a crash.

We still had only one bathroom.

BARBECUE

We had a huge barbecue pit. It looked like a fort. In fact, we mainly used it to play fort. It loomed over the patio—an enormous pile of brick featuring two ovens, both with iron doors, surrounding a big open area with a grate over it, and, topping the whole thing, a chimney which looked like something you'd see on a foundry. The chimney part was probably intended for smoking hams, but we used it to play factory. The ovens weren't useful to anybody but Harry Falk, who shut Ray up in one.

We almost never barbecued in the barbecue, because it was just too big.

The last time I saw the barbecue used as a barbecue was one spring day when my mother's old roommate, Mary Eunice, came through town. Mary Eunice was responsible for inviting Mama to the party where my parents had met, so they weren't sparing any effort to entertain her. My mother made a salad with three kinds of lettuce, which Granny thought was overkill. "Old expensive mess," she muttered, and promptly got sent down the street to spend the day with Mrs. Pilson.

I had never seen Mama so dressed up on a Saturday afternoon. She wore a dress with a big full skirt and high heels in which she teetered uncertainly around the yard. My father, who was wearing shorts, mostly supervised Lee, who was in charge of the actual barbecuing.

Lee's full name was Asa Lee Carter. Lee was married to Robert, our yard man who spent most of his weekends in jail. She had done our laundry in a galvanized tub in the yard until we got a washing machine. After that, in addition to helping Robert, she was promoted to barbecuer, which involved a lot less work. Lee was big and jolly. I once asked her why she was black. "Because," she said proudly, "I is chocolate." This didn't make much sense, but I left it alone.

The morning of the Mary Eunice barbecue, my father had gone extra early to pick Lee up from her little house off the Old Selma Road. As soon as she arrived, Lee lined the barbecue pit with foil, filled it with a whole sack of charcoal briquets and lit them, then stood there fanning the fire with a newspaper. I stood by to help her. "You ever know," asked Lee, taking a break to fan herself, "how to catch a witch?" Lee was full of good information. Apparently this sort of witch, which had nothing to do with Halloween, was a major hazard on the Old Selma Road. A witch, continued Lee, was somebody who could take her skin off, after which she became invisible and able to go around at night causing trouble. To catch a witch, you waited until it was dark, then went to the suspected witch's house and broke in. "What happens if she's home?" I asked.

"Then," said Lee judiciously, "you runs." Assuming the witch wasn't home, you looked under the bed and got the witch's skin, which would be rolled up like a throw rug. You hid it, and then when the witch came in after her nightly rampage, she would be unable to find her skin and would run around helplessly looking for it until the sun came up, at which time she would die. I had all kinds of questions, like how you could make sure she was dead if you couldn't see her, but I heard the bus pulling up.

33

Libby, whose mission today was to stop Ray and Clay from running into the street, got off the bus, and I ran up the driveway to greet her.

Mama and I were in the kitchen making the potato salad when I heard brakes screeching and Libby yelling "Come back out of that street!" It turned out that Mary Eunice had arrived in a taxi. We met her coming up the driveway right behind Libby, who was dragging Ray and Clay.

Mary Eunice was a tiny woman who looked sort of like a bird. She had a tuft of blonde curls and little beady eyes. She was wearing black pedal pushers, a white blouse with a frilly collar, big gold earrings, and high-heel sandals. I already knew that Mary Eunice had married an air force captain whom she had met at that same party, and that she had, as Mama had said excitedly, lived all over the world. Mary Eunice was very enthusiastic about meeting us, though I probably made a better impression than Ray and Clay, who were still being restrained by Libby. Mama took Mary Eunice into the backyard to have Cokes on the patio with my father, and I went back in the house.

I found Lee in the kitchen mixing up something which she then smeared on a large slab of meat. "What's that?" I asked, pointing to the slab.

"That spareribs," said Lee. I thought she was saying sparrow ribs. "Huh," I thought, "probably some expensive sort of sparrow."

It took a while for the ribs to cook. Lee had to lean way over the blazing-hot grill to flip them over and baste them; she paused occasionally to mop her face with her apron. Finally, the ribs were done and Lee heaved them onto a big platter. Libby reappeared, dragging Ray and carrying Clay, and plopped both of them down at the picnic table.

For a little woman, Mary Eunice had a hearty appetite, though she did daintily blot her mouth with her napkin between ribs. "These," she said, "are just too, too delicious." She was really eating a lot of ribs.

I ran off to report to Lee, who was eating ribs in the garage with Libby. "Mary Eunice is eating all your ribs," I said. "That what she sposed to do," said Lee. I turned to Libby, who was sitting on an upturned tub. "Why are you sitting on a tub?" I asked.

"You eat too much barbecue," intoned Libby, "and you end up sitting on the tub." Lee thought this was a lot funnier than I did.

34

"You know," added Lee, "how to make somebody into a zombie?" Libby and I were both interested, though I needed clarification. "What's a zombie?"

"A zombie," said Lee, "is somebody dead who has to do everything you say."

"Huh," said Libby, obviously impressed. I thought somebody alive who had to do everything you say might be more useful. Lee polished off a rib before continuing. "When you make somebody into a zombie," she said, "you got to throw goofer dust on them." Libby nodded. "You can throw it, put it in their food, or put it under the doorstep."

"What's goofer dust?" I asked, wondering if you threw it on them before or after they died.

Libby already knew this part. "Goofer dust," she said, "that dirt out of the graveyard." Lee nodded somberly. At this, the conversation veered off into mutual friends of Lee and Libby who had recently died—without, as far as I could tell, being turned into zombies—so I wandered off. I spent most of the rest of the day playing hide-and-go-seek with Ray and Clay, since the barbecue pit was still too hot to touch.

That night I heard my parents talking about the barbecue pit. "It just doesn't work," said my mother. "We can't even use it by ourselves." My father made a noise which sounded like agreement.

I didn't have much time to worry about the future of the barbecue pit—and in fact it was so big that I didn't think there was any chance of my parents being able to get rid of it unless they hired a steam shovel—because my birthday was just around the corner. I knew Ray and Clay were getting me a pool float, since I had found it, but I was in the dark about what my main present would be. I already had a Barbie.

The morning of my birthday I came running into the living room to find—along with the pool float—a record player complete with a Davy Crockett record, some assorted Barbie clothes, and a book about dinosaurs. This was pretty good, but apparently there was more in store. "Your big present," said my mother, beaming, "is out in the backyard." This was a little alarming. What if it was a horse? I was scared of horses.

It wasn't a horse. There on the patio stood a barbecue grill—the metal kind, with wheels—topped with a pink bow.

"Wowww!" I yelled, in unison with Ray and Clay. I had never even heard of anybody getting an entire barbecue grill for her birthday, much less someone my age. It was almost like getting a helicopter.

Even Granny seemed to like it. At any rate, she didn't say anything about it. "Can we cook on it? Huh?" we all yelled.

In fact, we cooked on it for my birthday that night. My father dumped a bag of charcoal into the grill, then poured a can of lighter fluid over it. Then I was sent with Ray and Clay out to the front yard, so that in case the grill blew up, the only people killed would be our parents. We sat on the curb in suspense for about ten minutes, then since we hadn't heard an explosion, we ventured into the backyard, where my father was poking the fire with a stick. My mother went in the house and came back with a plate full of hamburger patties, which we piled on the grill. Granny peered at the grill, muttered unintelligibly and retreated to the picnic table.

After we finished the hamburgers, we toasted marshmallows on coat hangers. The fastest way to do this, I discovered, was to set your marshmallow on fire.

Even though it had been a spectacular birthday, I lay awake for a while that night.

I doubted the new barbecue grill was big enough for sparrow ribs. What would Lee do? I already knew that Libby would be leaving as soon as her grandmother died, though her grandmother seemed to be taking her time about it. Since there wasn't any laundry or barbecuing for her to do, would Lee leave?

The next Saturday, Lee arrived just as usual. "Come on!" I yelled, as she got out of the car. "Come see my new barbecue grill!"

Lee appeared to like the grill as much as I did. She walked around it, admiring it from all angles. "We've already been cooking hamburgers," I said, before I could stop myself.

"Say you have?" said Lee. She thought a moment, then sat down in a patio chair, which creaked, and eased off her shoes. "You ever know," she asked, "about what you do if you sees a hoop snake?"

VACATION BIBLE SCHOOL

Vacation Bible School was better than real school. It lasted only two weeks, Morningview Baptist Church was air-conditioned, and they let you wear shorts. For the first day of Bible school, I had on red shorts, a blue top with a boat on it, and scuffed white sandals that I planned to get rid of as soon as nobody was looking. It was early June, but at 8:00 A.M. it was already hot. It didn't help that we were all lined up on the church's asphalt parking lot. The whole place smelled like tar. Although the church had been taking up money to buy a steeple ever since I could remember, they still didn't have enough: the building looked like a big brick box. The best thing about the church was the flower bed out front, which had big Spanish dagger plants—useful if you happened to get into a swordfight.

I had just turned eight, but I was an old hand at Vacation Bible School. As I waited for the big kid to blow the bugle, indicating that we were free to charge into the building, I thought back to my early years in Bible school, and the business venture I had started. One Sunday I had been standing idly outside the boys' bathroom, waiting for Ray and Clay to come out, when I started wondering why a church that couldn't even afford a steeple would bother paying for two bathrooms. After all, at home we had one bathroom for six people. It wouldn't surprise me, I thought, if the boys' bathroom had features the girls' bathroom lacked. When I investigated, I found my suspicions entirely justified. Then I had an inspiration. "People," I thought, inspecting the urinal, "would pay good money to see this."

In fact, every little girl in the class—and even some of the boys— had lined up to pay me a nickel for the guided tour. My commentary drew them in, especially the grand finale, when, indicating the urinal, I would declaim "and this is where they pee!" Everything was going so well, until somebody told.

I couldn't imagine why my parents were upset. I had made nearly four dollars—in fact, my business was going so much better than any of my father's projects, which generally lost money. I had finally been forced to bring the discussion to an end by announcing, "Well, I'm tired of hearing about it," which is what my mother always said.

I sighed. My short-lived tour business was probably the only interesting thing that would ever happen at Bible school.

Just then the bugle blew and we all ran into the building.

Starting at juice break, things did actually begin to get interesting. I had lined up to get my paper cup with Lorraine Key and Candace Sorrell. They were both famous, though for different reasons. Lorraine was famous for living right across the street from the church. She was almost never late for Sunday school. Candace was famous because her mother had been killed when a stove exploded. I was absolutely horrified by this information. I was also pretty curious as to what her mother had been trying to cook. I thought maybe I should find out so that my mother wouldn't try to cook it. Today both Candace and Lorraine were pointing at a new girl who was standing off to one side. Early that morning, I had noticed the thin dark-haired girl lined up with the fourth graders. As we stood around drinking Welch Ade, word filtered through the parking lot that the girl's name was Estella and that she spoke Spanish. Candace and Lorraine were all over this information. "Estella! How do you say 'damn'?" Estella thought. "Caramba!" she reported.

Estella turned out to be a gold mine of vocabulary improvement, but before she could answer a query relating to "son of a bitch," the bugle blew and we had to go back inside. As we settled into our chairs, our teacher, Mrs. Patterson, walked to the front of the room, beaming. Mrs. Patterson had curly black hair and wore red lipstick which matched her earrings and the cherry print on her full-skirted dress. She was always trying to get me, Lorraine, and Candace to use the Easy-Bake Oven, in which none of us had the slightest interest. Now she was holding up a big box labeled "Craft Projects." We were going to make something, she announced enthusiastically. The girls were going to cross-stitch potholders. She held up a small, limp, beige potholder. The boys, she continued, would paint cutting boards. She brandished one. These cutting boards, easily a foot long, were shaped like paddles—just the right size for an impressive painting. Furthermore, after the boys finished painting them, the cutting boards would be varnished by Mrs. Patterson's husband, since, as Mrs. Patterson put it, she didn't know the first thing about varnishing. I waved my hand. Mrs. Patterson, who clearly remembered me from the bathroom-tour days, frowned. I didn't let it stop me. "Mrs. Patterson," I said, "the girls want to do cutting boards too." "Yeah," said Lorraine Key and Candace Sorrell.

Mrs. Patterson appeared horrified. "But don't you want to learn how to sew?"

"We already know how to sew."

"Yeah."

Mrs. Patterson fanned herself. The situation was saved by the other teacher, Mrs. Rowell. Mrs. Rowell was taller and thinner than Mrs. Patterson, and her clothes weren't as frilly, but she was interesting because she was a British war bride. I didn't know what that meant, but Mrs. Rowell was clearly unusual and might, I thought, be sort of like Wonder Woman. Now she put her superhuman diplomatic skills to work and a compromise was reached. The girls would cross-stitch and paint cutting boards. There was some talk about letting the boys also cross-stitch, but there were no takers—proving, I thought, that cutting boards were better.

For the next week, Bible school hummed along happily. On juice breaks, Estella was generally available to work with us on our pronunciation, and we learned several useful phrases. Ray and Clay, whom I also saw on juice breaks, had discovered how to get into the sanctuary and were planning to explore the baptismal tank. I hoped they wouldn't try to start a tour business.

I learned all the books of the New Testament and finished my cross-stitched potholder in record time—no challenge, since I already had an apron and several pillowcases to my credit. Then Mrs. Patterson grudgingly handed out the cutting boards. What should I paint? Candace was doing a daisy, which was a good idea, but I didn't want to be derivative. Lorraine had gone with a cat. She had gotten carried away with the ears. The thing looked like the Easter rabbit. Whatever I did, I knew it would have to be good enough to squelch Mrs. Patterson's assumption that my painting skills weren't the equal of anyone's.

On the last day of Bible school, we always had hot dogs for lunch, after which our parents would load us and our craft projects into the car. I waved goodbye to Estella: "Adios!" I was going to add something about "puta grande" but her parents were there. My mother was talking with Mrs. Patterson. Mama was looking a little fidgety, probably because she had left my father trying to strike a jury by himself while she came to collect my brothers and me. I was concentrating on not spilling mustard on myself, but I did hear Mrs. Patterson say, "And for some reason I can't imagine, the girls wanted to do cutting boards too." I could feel her looking at me, but I didn't care. I smiled at my cutting board. I had painted a watermelon on it.

MOBILE

We were going through the Bankhead Tunnel, and I was having trouble holding my breath. I finally decided it was okay to stop. The air was full of diesel fumes, so it wasn't much different from not breathing.

We were headed to Gulf Shores, but first we were spending the night in Mobile with Mr. and Mrs. Nolte and their children, Helen and Timmy. My father had taught school years ago with Dan Nolte, and I'd met Ellie Nolte when she came to Montgomery to do research on her ancestors. She was a little gray-haired woman who talked nonstop. "I'm just having so much trouble," she had moaned, "with these pre-Revolutionary documents."

The Noltes' big white house stood on a dead-end street, surrounded by huge pines. Under the trees were mounds of azaleas full of red, purple, pink, and white flowers. The air held a faint fragrance; every time the breeze shifted, it was gone. I tried smelling an azalea but it wasn't the same. I decided it was the thousands of them, all blooming together, that produced this wispy flower scent, as if the air was different here.

While I was thinking this, Timmy and Helen wandered up. Helen was a pale, fat blonde girl. Timmy, who was one year older than me, was pale, too. His eyelashes were almost white. I gestured toward the garage. Mrs. Nolte had waved at the set of windows over it and called it the maid's quarters. "Should we go say hi to your maid?" I asked politely.

"Huh? Oh, Ida doesn't live there. There's nothing up there but a bunch of boxes of my mother's papers and stuff. She's in the DAR."

"Oh," I said. I didn't know what the DAR was.

"Yeah," he said. "She's always trying to trace her ancestors. She's got them traced all the way back to Attila the Hun on her mother's side, but she's having trouble with her father's. She says she's going to have to go back to Montgomery." At this point, Timmy spotted a bee on an azalea. "Bees!" he said, clearly alarmed. "Come on, let's get out of here!"

For supper, which Ellie Nolte called "dinner" and served in the dining room, we had chicken. Baked, not fried. We also had asparagus, which I'd never heard of, served with a thick yellow sauce that Ellie called hollandaise. Ray and Clay refused to eat it because they thought she had said mayonnaise. There were strawberries for dessert. Real ones, not frozen. All during the meal, Mr. Nolte tried to tell my father about the insurance business, but every time he opened his mouth, Mrs. Nolte would come out with some new information about how she was related to the king of Prussia.

After we ate, my father went outside with Mr. Nolte to look at Mr. Nolte's convertible, and Timmy, Ray, and Clay went in the den to watch *Highway Patrol.* Helen sat with Mama and me in the living room, which had a window seat, and listened to Mrs. Nolte talk about trying to prove that Cousin Walter had been in a Yankee prison camp from 1862 until late spring of 1865. Apparently the Yankees hadn't kept good records, especially compared to the Huns. Finally, Helen said, "Mama, I'm going to show Kathie the rest of the house." Mrs. Nolte, who was now talking about Martha Washington's sister-in-law, waved her hand in dismissal.

Helen's real plan turned out to be standing on a kitchen chair to get a bag of chocolate chip cookies out of the cabinet, but when Timmy, Ray, and Clay came in, she shrugged, handed us each a cookie, kept the rest of the bag, and headed down the hall, saying "Come on."

Helen's room was upstairs. I caught a glimpse of a white canopy bed and a white dresser. I thought enviously that Helen didn't have to share a room with her grandmother, which probably meant she didn't have a chamber pot under her bed either, but Helen didn't seem enthusiastic about me looking under there, so I didn't.

Timmy's room wasn't remarkable except that he had a collection of arrowheads and, on the wall, an autographed photo of Roy Rogers. It was signed "Your pal, Roy."

Ray and Clay were enchanted. "Wow!" said Ray. "Where'd you get it?"

Timmy shrugged. "Sent off for it," he said. "It came in the mail." I wondered why Roy had wanted to sign the photo "Your pal," when it was obvious he and Timmy didn't have much of a friendship.

That night, Mama and I slept in one of the Noltes' guest rooms with the windows open. I kept hearing a soothing noise, almost like something breathing outside. "What's that?" I asked Mama. "That's the wind," she said, "soughing in the branches of the pines."

"What's it doing?"

"Soughing."

"Oh."

The next day, we had waffles—another new experience—for breakfast, then headed to Gulf Shores. Mrs. Nolte was still talking as we backed down the driveway. Apparently, they were all coming to see us at the Gulf in a couple of days.

The weather at the beach was perfect, though one morning I got a very bad sunburn and took refuge under the cottage, where I sat, thinking. I had come up with a great idea. We had always known that if both my parents died, my brothers and I would go live with Mama's Cousin Emojean in Mississippi. Now, however, I had had an inspiration. If both my parents died, I would go live with the Noltes. If, I thought happily, Ray and Clay wanted to live with Cousin Emojean, that would be all right with me. I pictured myself moving into the Noltes' guestroom. They wouldn't even have to get me a canopy bed, unless they especially wanted to. Or—I had an even better thought— they could just move all those boxes out of the maid's quarters and I could live there. I pictured myself, sitting in a window seat, looking out the window at the azaleas, listening to the wind soughing while eating waffles.

The next day, the Noltes showed up. By the time they got there, I had already been swimming once but was ready to go again.

I was kind of surprised to see that Helen and Timmy were wearing big floppy hats, the kind my mother wore. At least they also had on swimsuits. "Come on!" I yelled. "Let's go swimming!"

I started to run down to the water. "Wait, wait!" yelled Timmy. "I haven't got on sunscreen."

"Mama's coming! Mama's coming," called Mrs. Nolte cheerfully, reaching into her big purse. "Everybody into the shade!" She opened a huge tube of zinc-oxide ointment. "Now stand still." She smeared the stuff all over Helen and Timmy. By the time she finished, they looked like they had been painted white. I wasn't sure I wanted to be seen with them. Mr. Nolte headed into the Gulf, waving at my father, and dove into the surf.

Helen wouldn't go in the water with us; in fact, she only stayed on the beach about five minutes, after which she went to sit on the porch. Timmy and I waded into the Gulf, which was calm. "Come on," I said, "don't you want to go out to the sandbar?"

I gestured farther out to where Mr. Nolte, Ray, Clay, and my father were walking around in knee-deep water.

He shook his head. "I'm not allowed out there. There's an undertow." Then he jumped. "Ow!" "What?" I said, looking around for sharks. "A jellyfish! It got on me!" Timmy headed for the shore. I shrugged and followed him. Helen was fanning herself and eating a Fudgsicle. She had broken out in purple welts. "Poor Helen," Mrs. Nolte was saying. "She's allergic to almost everything. Helen, don't eat that Popsicle."

"It's a Fudgsicle," said Helen indistinctly, but she stopped eating it. "I just know it was those strawberries," Mrs. Nolte continued. "A delayed reaction. Dr. Mitchell said that happens sometimes. Here, Helen, take your Benadryl. Do you have any bottled water?" "Uh, no," said Mama, looking embarrassed.

"That's all right," said Mrs. Nolte. "I never travel without it." She rummaged in her purse and came out with a bottle. "Both the children have such trouble with tap water." Helen's welts didn't go away, so after a while Mrs. Nolte walked out to the beach where she stood waving and yelling "Dan! Yoo-hoo!" until Mr. Nolte, looking disappointed, came out of the water. They didn't stay for lunch, even though we were having hot dogs.

That night, my parents had an argument which started immediately after my mother's announcement that Ellie Nolte had invited herself to stay with us the following month while she did more research at the state archives. Their door was closed, but I heard my father say "known Dan since 1930," and my mother say "only one bathroom," "talk a blue streak," and, in a somewhat louder voice, "Attila the Hun."

The next day, my parents seemed to have made up, though every once in a while my mother said "Hmpf," which I interpreted to mean that Mrs. Nolte was coming to stay with us. We were all pretty subdued as we packed the car and climbed in, my mother slamming the door harder than usual.

The inside of the car was very hot, even with my head stuck out the window. As we drove up the highway, I could see water ahead, shimmering all across the road. "We're going to go through a lake," I said excitedly.

"That's not water," said my mother. "That's a mirage."

"What's a mirage?"

"A mirage is when you think something's real, but it isn't."

Sure enough, when we drove over the place I'd seen the lake, the pavement was dry.

It had looked exactly like water.

FLASH CARD

I usually had poached eggs for breakfast, partly because I liked the way they looked when they came out of the egg poacher. I also liked dumping them on toast and then sticking them with a fork. In fact, breakfast used to be fun, before the flash cards.

"Seven times six!" yelled my father, brandishing a flash card with "7 × 6" on it. "Uh," I said, "forty?"

"No! No! It's not forty! You just said seven times five is thirty-five! Seven times six couldn't possibly be forty!"

I tried to count. "Forty two?"

"That's right," said my father grudgingly. I took the opportunity to bite carefully into my poached egg before it got any colder.

"Eat your breakfast! Just eat it! You're like a mule eating briars!" I wasn't sure what a mule eating briars looked like, and at any rate the egg was now completely cold.

"May I be excused?" I asked.

"No! Finish that breakfast. Seven times seven!"

I wasn't the only one being harassed. Ray, who was in first grade, got spelling cards every time he turned around. Clay was still in kindergarten, and fortunately nobody had invented flash cards for bead stringing, but he still looked worried every time my father started screaming at Ray and me about how to spell *cow* or what was the capital of Idaho.

The problem was, there were too many of us. That's what all the teachers said every time I asked why we couldn't go on a field trip or make art projects, like the children did in our readers. Occasionally, the teacher might add, "Where do you think you are, private school?"

I was in third grade, but the school had combined us with fourth grade, which made forty of us packed solidly into one classroom. To top things off, we were expected to learn the multiplication table.

There were only two bright spots in the situation. One was that the school had decided that since there were too many of us, we would not be required to learn how to divide by fractions. When we grew up, said the teacher, if we needed something divided by a fraction, we should just ask someone. The other good thing was that frequently if Mrs. Lemley was busy teaching the fourth graders something, we could just sit there and color. It was almost like being in private school.

This in no way made up for the multiplication table, and, according to my father, the only way to learn multiplication or spelling was by constant practice. He had some experience in the area, since before going to law school he had been a teacher in a one-room school, where he had once whipped everybody in the class on the grounds that they had probably done something.

Since my father had lost his right arm, he couldn't wave a flash card and eat at the same time. This guaranteed me uninterrupted, if brief, stretches at breakfast during which I could take a gingerly bite or two of toast, though my father was apt to fire off spelling words at Ray during the lull. At any rate, my breakfast was still disrupted by my mother and Granny, who would criticize me for not eating. "You don't eat enough to keep a bird alive," said Mama. "You're going to die of some terrible disease." I wondered if there was such a thing as egg deficiency.

Granny, meanwhile, would be trying to get me to put gravy on something and pointing out that she had been told frequently that I would die in infancy. I wasn't sure who had told her this, but it may have been her Sunday school class.

Eventually, my father figured out that he wasn't getting our undivided attention, so he decided that flash cards would take place after supper. This guaranteed a little more peace at meals, though the new schedule interfered to a great extent with watching television. I went weeks without getting to see *Walt Disney's Wonderful World of Color.*

As the school year wound down, all the grades had tests pretty much nonstop, and worrying about multiplication took up a good deal of my time. Specifically, I wasn't sure what happened after nine times nine. The tens would be easy, but then what? One night, I had a dream in which Nikita Khrushchev was interrogating me: "Twelve times eleven! Answer the question!"

I was also worried about Ray, who, I thought, was not taking spelling seriously enough. At his age, I had brooded for days after leaving out the second *p* in *pumpkin,* but there were weeks when he didn't even bother learning his spelling words, telling my father that the teacher hadn't assigned any.

"What," I asked, "are you gonna do when you have to learn the multiplication table?" Ray shrugged.

He probably figured that by the time he was in third grade, there would be so many students that they wouldn't have to learn anything at all.

One spring day, I was walking home, trying to remember what eight times nine was. I passed the Bronson house, which was dark. Celia Bronson was on another one of her mysterious trips out of town, and apparently the little boy people called her brother was being kept inside by her elderly parents. All thought of the Bronsons left me when I saw Ray playing in the drainage ditch across from Harry Falk's house. "What are you doing?" I asked. "Aren't you supposed to have a spelling test tomorrow?"

Ray snorted. "Who cares?" he said, and with that he actually threw his spelling book and all his papers into the drainage ditch, where they made an impressive pile.

I was horrified. "Don't do that!" I yelled. Ray started laughing. Dickie Pate, who was walking by, gave us a funny look. "I'm going to Dickie's," continued Ray. Dickie gave us another funny look, but shrugged as Ray, still laughing, fell in beside him.

There I was, standing beside a drainage ditch full of books and papers, some of which were starting to blow away. I was frozen for a minute, but then I mechanically set down my own books, crawled down into the ditch, which had briers in it, and began picking up Ray's stuff, crying my eyes out.

The worst part was, I had no idea why I was doing it.

At home, I threw Ray's stuff on his bed where my father wouldn't see that his books had dirt on them, and went across to Patty Harris's. "I hate school," I said. "Me too," said Patty, adding that Sister Evangelista had recently locked her in a closet for chewing gum. This cheered me up, so I went home.

I glared at Ray all through supper, but he didn't seem to notice. He and Clay were preoccupied with not getting caught for failure to drink their milk. They both had a fear of milk, which they claimed had pieces of wax from the carton in it. "Drink that milk!" yelled my father. "Who has a test tomorrow?" "Ray has a spelling test," I announced happily. Ray glared at me. "All right," said my father, "after supper we're doing flash cards."

We all went in the living room for flash cards. Clay looked sadly at the television set. "Can I go to Bobby's?" he asked. "No," said my father. "Pay attention and learn something. Spell 'chair,'" he added to Ray.

Ray got through *chair, wolf,* and *hall,* but then the trouble started. "Spell 'milk.'"

"M-L-I-K," said Ray confidently.

"No! Spell 'milk!'"

"M-L-I-K?" repeated Ray. Clay started turning pale. Granny, who probably couldn't spell *milk* either, went out in the hall. My mother, who was sitting by me on the couch, wet her lips nervously.

"Milk! Spell 'milk'! Can't you even spell 'milk'?"

"I-M-L-K?"

My father grabbed Ray and dragged him onto the enclosed porch. There was the sound of a slap, then a thud.

Mama got up from the couch. "Don't you hit that child," she said, under her breath. I could hardly hear her. Clay got behind the couch.

"K-L-I-M!" yelled Ray, sounding desperate.

I went out in the garage. It was dark out there, and under other circumstances I might have thought it was scary. I sat on the car bumper. "Seven times seven," I said. "Seven times eight. Seven times nine."

SCOUTS

I had learned how to cook a couple of things from Granny, but she didn't know how to fix anything that you didn't fry. I asked Mama if she could teach me how to cook. "What do you want to know that for?" she asked suspiciously. As we talked, she was dumping ground meat into a bowl and mashing cornflakes into it.

"What's that?" I asked.

"Meatloaf," said Mama wearily, reaching for an onion. "Why do you want to learn to cook?"

"Well," I said, "I thought it might be fun."

"You wouldn't think it was fun," said Mama, pouring ketchup into the bowl, "if you had to do it every day."

She had a point, but I thought her attitude toward the kitchen might really have stemmed from unfamiliarity. Before she married at the age of thirty, my mother had lived in a boardinghouse where meals and laundry were provided. Her Aunt Katherine had taught her to bake a coconut cake, but that was her only domestic skill. In a kitchen drawer, my mother kept a little book entitled *A Lawyer's Calendar* that an insurance company had sent her. She pasted recipes and household hints from the paper in it. One of the pages, originally headed "Arraignments," now featured an article called "How to Use an Electric Washing Machine."

Even if my mother had liked cooking, she would have found it hard to endure comments from Granny, who was a severe food critic. Following one of the newspaper's recipes, my mother had once put bay leaves into a stew. "Stick them old leaves in everything," Granny had muttered, believing that my mother had just gone out in the yard and pulled leaves off the hackberry tree.

I still thought I should learn something about cooking, and it was about this time that I saw a poster at school for Girl Scouts. "Join the Fun!" it said, over a drawing of a girl toasting a marshmallow at a campfire. I could learn to cook and set things on fire at the same time!

My mother agreed that it would be a good idea for me to join the scouts. "I was a Campfire Girl," she said, "but we didn't really do anything except sing. It would be good for you to learn something useful."

The Cloverdale Girl Scout troop met after school at the home of Jenny Craven, right across the street from the school. Mrs. Craven had time to be a troop leader because she didn't work, but it turned out she didn't cook or do housework either. Once we built a fire in her barbecue pit, and I did learn how to make s'mores, but that was the only cooking we did. Other than that, we spent the meetings looking at Mrs. Craven's clothes, which were pretty spectacular, or watching Janie, the maid, iron, or reading Jenny's stacks of comic books. Every week, we took turns bringing refreshments. None of the other girls had mothers who worked, except for Sarah Stein, whose mother helped run Stein Art Supplies. Though there was never much going on at the actual meeting, our snacks could get pretty elaborate. Betsy Gant's mother once showed up with homemade sugar cookies with our names written on them in icing. Everybody liked them almost as much as the Krispy Kreme donuts that Sarah's mother brought.

One week I noticed a huge stack of boxes on Jenny's sunporch. "It's Girl Scout Cookie Time!" said Mrs. Craven gaily. "We're all going to sell cookies to help out the troop."

I tried going around with Sarah to sell cookies, though this didn't work very well because we'd inevitably get hungry and end up just eating them. However, I managed to sell fifty boxes by hanging around my parents' office and harassing all their clients and the people who worked in the other offices.

Sarah sold seventy-five boxes. That wasn't really a fair test since at least twenty were to herself, but, regardless, she and I were the top producers in the troop. Next time it was her turn for refreshments, Sarah just brought in a whole carton of Thin Mints.

Ironically, this was the last good snack we had.

After the cookie sale died down, I noticed something weird going on with the troop refreshments. President Kennedy had announced his physical fitness program, which meant we had to spend recess doing jumping jacks. This was bad enough, but apparently some of the troop mothers had interpreted physical fitness to mean we shouldn't have anything that tasted good for refreshments. Instead of donuts or cupcakes, girls in the troop started showing up with really dry homemade oatmeal cookies. The low point was reached when Bonnie Britton, whose mother was a Yankee, brought carrot sticks with yogurt dip. We didn't have soft drinks anymore; apple juice was as good as it got. The only bright spot was when it was Jenny's turn, and Mrs. Craven just had the cook, Ethel, make a pound cake. "After all," I heard her telling Bonnie's mother, "it is homemade."

The most humiliating thing that could happen to a person in the troop was forgetting when it was her turn to do refreshments. This happened to Becca Hollis. We were learning about embroidery hoops when I saw her go pale. "Oh no!" she said. "I forgot refreshments." Mrs. Craven waved in the direction of the pantry. "Go use the phone," she said. Apparently Mrs. Hollis was still in bed, but Becca persuaded her older half-brother to bring food; he showed up with a bag of Fritos and a watermelon. The following week it was Sarah Stein's turn again and we had whole-wheat bagels. "These donuts are really bad," said someone accusingly.

Whenever my mother asked me how scouts was going, I assumed she was asking about what we were eating. "Well," I said one Thursday, "We had Jello." I wasn't crazy about Jello but at least it didn't involve raw vegetables. Unfortunately, all this talk of refreshments had awakened Mama's competitive instinct: she decided to prove she could cook. "Jello," said my mother, with a faraway look. "I could make Jello. I'm sure I could." Except for Christmas and Easter, when Mama made the coconut cake, dessert at our house was usually store-bought cinnamon rolls or Colonial Creme-filled Cupcakes. After that week's trip to Kwik-Chek, however, Mama made blackberry Jello. Unfortunately, something went wrong; it didn't solidify. "Hmpf," said Granny, surveying the black liquid. "Old mess." My mother retreated to her room with a migraine headache, and my father threw a plate at Granny.

After that, whenever Mama asked me how scouts was going, I reported things that didn't involve cooking, like the time Becca fell into Mrs. Craven's lily pond, or our efforts to try on all Mrs. Craven's evening dresses. She had a whole huge closet of them. It took us two full meetings to try them all on; there should have been a merit badge.

Merit badges were on my mind because Patty Harris and Annette DeSalvo, both of whom belonged to the scout troop at Our Lady Queen of Sorrows, were earning them by doing things like identifying wildlife and camping out. I was a little less envious after Annette reported that their camping trip had ended with everyone sleeping in the car to avoid a herd of rabid raccoons. At least their snacks were no better than ours—Patty said they usually just had raw apples.

Meanwhile, our troop refreshments seemed about to get even worse; Patty's mother, who was crazy, gave a recipe to my mother for some sort of snack that featured yogurt, raisins, and shredded wheat.

Then, the week after we finally finished trying on Mrs. Craven's dresses, I arrived at scouts a little late to find everybody looking at me expectantly. A growing sense of horror crept over me. It was my turn for refreshments, meaning it was Mama's turn for refreshments.

"Uh," I said. "Can I use your phone?"

My mother answered the phone on the first ring. "Law office."

"Uh," I said, "Mama, it's my turn for refreshments at scouts."

"What? I'll be darned! I'll just be darned! Why didn't you tell me it was your turn? I was going to try to make something! Now I'll just have to go to Liger's!" The phone went dead.

"She'll be right here," I said brightly. "Can I look at your evening shoes again?"

Even though Mrs. Craven's evening shoes took up a whole closet, we had pretty much tried them all on by the time my mother arrived. Finally, the car pulled up in the driveway, the door flew open and my mother stumbled out. She was wearing a stylish plum-colored suit and high heels. Mrs. Craven, who, despite her extensive wardrobe was wearing pedal pushers, looked a little uncomfortable.

"I'm sorry," said my mother, out of breath, to Mrs. Craven. "This was all I could get."

Out came a case of Cokes and a large white box labeled "Liger's Premium Bakery."

"I've got to get back," added my mother distractedly, running a hand through her hair. Her gold earrings glinted. She gave me a tragic look, climbed back in the car and roared out of the driveway in the direction of downtown.

I set the Cokes down on the ground and opened the box. Two dozen fudge brownies, with frosting.

"Wow," said Sarah Stein.

SAINT AUGUSTINE

This summer, things were going to be different. For one thing, my half-sister Mona wouldn't be going on vacation with us. I had phoned my parents' office after school one spring day, and my mother had answered. "Your daddy is real upset," she whispered. In the background, I could hear yelling, punctuated by a tremendous crash.

"Cammie called and said Mona's getting married."

This was a surprise. Who would marry Mona?

Once my father calmed down about the wedding (and about the fact that Cammie, his ex-wife, had erroneously thought he would pay for part of it), he announced that, for our summer vacation, we would go to Saint Augustine, Florida.

I was very excited. For one thing, Saint Augustine was the oldest city in the United States. For another thing, it was on the Atlantic Ocean, which should be a step up from the Gulf of Mexico.

It took a very long time to get to Saint Augustine. Fortunately, there was more room than usual in the car, since we didn't have Mona, and Granny had been sent off to Mrs. Pilson's. Ray and Clay and I celebrated by climbing back and forth over the seats.

Florida, it turned out, was full of opportunities to stop and see weird things. We drove right past an alligator farm and something called a snake-a-torium.

I was beginning to think we were never going to stop and see the sights, but then we spotted the most interesting sign yet: "Ponce de Leon Fountain of Youth." Obviously, this was worth seeing, even though it turned out to be more like a water fountain. There was a big painting of Ponce de Leon discovering the fountain on the wall behind it, and in the next room was Ponce de Leon's coffin. I was a little worried about this coffin and couldn't understand why they hadn't just buried him. I also wondered what he died of, since it couldn't have been old age.

My qualms about this coffin were completely overshadowed, however, by what happened next. We went into an innocuous-looking building that resembled a barn. The sign out front said "Florida's History Revealed!" Once we got inside, however, it turned out somebody had dug up a graveyard and there we were, on a viewing platform, looking down at all these skeletons. "Here we go again," I thought. "They've got some sort of objection to just burying people."

I was completely mystified. The sign said all these people were Indians. I didn't see what that had to do with it. One skeleton had a tiny skeleton lying next to it. A mother and baby, somebody whispered. This was the last straw. I was terrified of skeletons and had not yet gotten over the time Tommy Turner had brought one to first grade for show-and-tell.

And that was just one, not a whole room.

I went outside and sat on a fence. By the time Ray and Clay emerged, I had gotten to the point of being able to close my eyes without seeing the baby skeleton. Ray asked if I wanted to look at his postcards. I said no.

Saint Augustine, when we finally got there, had a couple of features I liked. One was the fort, which had cannons and was made entirely of little shells. It was conveniently located near a big amusement park. I also liked our cottage, which was under pine trees down the road from the beach.

The beach, however, was another story. I was used to the snow-white Gulf beaches. This beach was yellow, and the Atlantic was gray and colder than the Gulf. One day, I wandered down to the beach looking for shells. I didn't find any. When I got back to the cottage, I found my mother obviously annoyed about something. It turned out to be Ray and Clay, who were complaining about sandspurs. Coincidentally, I had just been complaining about the same thing. "When I was little," said my mother, angrily slamming a frying pan down on the stove, "the only beach I had to go to was Biloxi, and it was full of sandspurs, but I never complained." At this point, my father entered. "Guess what?" he said jovially.

"WHAT???" demanded my mother.

My father looked affronted. "I'm not going to tell you, if you act that way about it."

Since the situation was deteriorating, I left.

It was about time for the mail. Though we'd only been in Saint Augustine for a few days, I had developed a routine. Early in the afternoon, I would go to the cottage office to see if there was any mail for Farnell. There never was. My errand was complicated by the fact that the man in charge of the cottages was deaf and dumb. I supposed my father must have made our reservations in writing. I climbed up the steps to the office, waved to get the man's attention, and held up a piece of paper with "Any Mail for Farnell?" written on it. The man, who was old and bald, shook his head, and then, to clarify matters, held up a piece of paper with "No Mail Today" written on it.

When I got back to the cottage, my mother had calmed down and put away the frying pan. We were, my father announced, going to go to the amusement park and—he glanced at my mother—get hamburgers instead of cooking supper.

This was more like it. The hamburgers were not bad, and the amusement park itself was right on the beach and had a long pier. The most interesting ride was the swings. These looked like ordinary swings, but they were rocket-powered or something, because when you started swinging on them, it was possible to go all the way over the top bar and down again, just like on a Ferris wheel. I watched for a while to see if anybody would fall off, but nobody did. "Let's go," said my father. "We're going in the store." There was a big souvenir store right next to the park. I supposed I could get some postcards, unless they had snow globes. I was shaking a snow globe with a flamingo in it when my mother said "Ray?"

I looked around. Ray, who had been right there looking at a dried seahorse, wasn't there. Clay was still around, sitting on a shelf next to a sand bucket. "Where's Ray?" asked my mother. Clay just shook his head. "Ray!" bellowed my father. Clay immediately vanished into the depths of the shelf, pulling the bucket in front of him like a hermit crab. I dropped to the floor and covered my head with my arms.

54

When I got up and dusted myself off, a few people were looking at us. I thought for sure we'd find Ray in the bathroom, or at the display of porcupine fish, but we didn't. It was getting dark outside. At this point, the store manager came up, talked to my parents for a minute, then went away, coming back almost immediately with a man in a uniform.

"Who's that?" I asked my mother. "Deputy sheriff," she said. She had turned pale. "Ray!" roared my father. This time, everyone in the store turned and looked. I leaned over and peered beneath the shelf. I could barely see Clay. "Come on out," I said. He shook his head. The store manager came back over. "The sheriff's got all the men out looking for him," he said soothingly. "The best thing is for y'all to go back to your cottage, and the sheriff will bring him straight to y'all." My mother nodded. "Come on," she said. Clay crawled out from under the shelf. When we got out the door, my father yelled "Ray!" one more time, but it was obvious his heart wasn't in it. We were nearly across the parking lot when the sheriff's car pulled up. The sheriff, smiling broadly, climbed out, holding Ray, who was clutching his postcards and looking uncertain. "Here you go!" said the sheriff happily. "Caught him wandering off down the road going thataway. He was even headed in the right direction." "Oh, Ray," said my mother, bursting into tears. The sheriff drove off, waving. My father grabbed Ray's shirt and started dragging him toward the water. "Ramon," said my mother, "can't we just go back to the—"

"Come here!" said my father, jerking Ray. He dragged him the length of the pier, with us following uncertainly.

"See that water?" said my father. It was pitch black, so nobody saw anything, but he pointed anyway. "If you run off again, I'm going to throw you off this pier and drown you."

Ray wailed. Clay wailed. My mother looked frozen. "I'm going to go sit in the car," I said to her. I didn't want to be accused of running off.

I leaned out the car window, watching the people on the swings. This was a good amusement park, but I couldn't say much for the rest of Saint Augustine. So far, this vacation was nothing but me and my brothers complaining, my mother slamming frying pans around, and my father threatening to kill people. Even if you didn't count the skeletons, which I did, it was no better than Montgomery.

Next year, I thought, we should just go back to Gulf Shores.

ADVENTURE

When I was sick in bed, my mother would bring me library books. This happened a lot, because I was always coming down with bronchitis. The doctor said I was allergic to dust. It could have been worse, I thought. I could have been allergic to air. My mother was usually in a hurry when she got to the library, so she just grabbed whatever books were on the New Books shelf, whether they were novels, cookbooks, or government training pamphlets. I knew more about industrial ceramics that any other nine-year-old in the country. One fall day, after flipping disinterestedly through *Care of the Silkworm*, which I had already read, I was happy to see she had brought the Roy Chapman Andrews book. I had also read the Roy Chapman Andrews book—in fact I had read it twenty or thirty times—but that didn't matter, since it was my favorite book.

Roy Chapman Andrews had gone to Outer Mongolia hunting dinosaur fossils about 1920 and had survived to write a book about his adventures. It was a great book, and I had read it so many times my mother even knew where to find it in the library. My favorite chapter depicted Roy Chapman Andrews finding a nest of dinosaur eggs. I had tried to recreate the incident by making dinosaur eggs out of Play-Doh but had been frustrated by the fact that you had to use a whole can per egg, and by my suspicion that dinosaur eggs were not bright pink.

If I wanted to do something adventurous once I got well, it was obvious I was going to have to look beyond Roy Chapman Andrews. Luckily about the time I resumed my regular schedule the Clover Theater's Kiddie Matinee was showing a series of episodes of *Tarzan and the River of Gold*. I was impressed by the scene in which some irate gold prospectors, chasing Tarzan through the jungle with machine guns, happen to fall into a pit lined with stakes that was meant for lions. "This is great!" I said, poking Ray. "We should play 'Tarzan.'" Ray looked dubious. "Where are we supposed to get a lion?"

Actually, I had been thinking more in terms of Patty Harris. She always showed up when it was least convenient, and had a bad habit of following people.

Sort of like a lion.

Our garage came equipped with a lot of shovels, hoes, and picks which had formerly been used on my grandparents' farm. "We can dig the pit right here," I said, indicating the sandbox. Ray and Clay shrugged and started digging. We dug the hole down about two feet, after which we got bored. At this point a basic flaw in the plan emerged. "We don't have any stakes," said Ray.

"Huh," I said. Then I noticed the rosebush.

It wasn't exactly the same, but we got the thorny limbs arranged, covered the pit with newspaper and sprinkled sand on it. Patty was in the habit of picking these small white flowers that grew in bunches in the grass, so we put some of them in the middle of the trap. Now all we had to do was wait.

Sure enough, about two minutes later, there was Patty.

"Hi Patty," I said casually. "You want to pick some flowers?"

Patty eyed me suspiciously. I realized I had tipped her off by not telling her to get lost.

"Okay," I said, trying to regroup. "Since you're here, I guess you can stay. But you better not pick any of my flowers here."

Ray spoiled the effect by weighing in. "Pick the flowers. I ain't got all day."

Patty folded her arms. "No," she said.

I considered just grabbing her and throwing her into the pit, but this would inevitably lead to her telling. We wound up playing on the swings instead: a complete waste of time.

The following Saturday, the Kiddie Matinee gave up on Tarzan and showed a movie called *King Solomon's Mines*. These mines were home to a huge series of tunnels which had, unfortunately, been dug too close to a volcano. At one point, the hero and his party find themselves sealed up inside the mines, but they escape by following an underground stream.

We didn't have a volcano, but when it came to tunnels and underground streams, we had the next best thing.

The storm drain.

This storm drain started behind Huntingdon College and ran under Fairview Avenue and the Cloverdale School football field. In fact, if you stayed in it long enough you would probably either surface somewhere near our house, or fall in the river. Access to the storm drain was easy; in the ditch where it started, it was high enough to walk into, though you had to stoop.

I immediately announced an expedition to the furthest reaches of the storm drain. This idea was popular with everybody who heard about it, except Patty Harris.

When we assembled at the storm drain, our group included Ellis and Till Chalmers. Till was Clay's age and, like Clay, seldom said anything. Ellis was Ray's age and had the advantage of actually having gone in the storm drain and living to tell about it.

"Okay," I said. "Has everybody got their candles and flashlights?"

Everybody had, and Ellis also had a butcher knife and a football helmet; I didn't want to ask why.

Just as we were getting ready to enter the drain, Till unexpectedly spoke up. "I ain't going in there," he said. "There's porcupines in there."

This was unwelcome news. "Aw," said Ellis, waving his butcher knife, "that's just what people say. I've been all in there and I didn't see any porcupines."

"They throw quills," added Till.

"You go first," I told Ellis.

Ellis shrugged, clapped his football helmet on, and headed into the dark. Till, after a little discussion, decided that he would come with us rather than be left alone at the entrance. There had been some controversy as to whether we should use the candles or the flashlights first. The candles had won on the grounds that you could write your name on the ceiling with the smoke. When the drain got too narrow to stand up, we would switch to flashlights. "Come on, men," said Ellis, pretty needlessly since we were right behind him. I was a little annoyed. On the one hand, he obviously felt that going first meant that he was now head of the expedition. On the other hand, what if there really were porcupines? I smiled grimly.

I really couldn't see much. The cement drainpipe formed the ceiling just over my head, and there was a little trickle of water on the ground that I tried to avoid. The walls were sort of damp. At least it wasn't dusty. The candles flickered; I had to be careful not to burn the person in front of me, and to avoid getting hot wax on me. Behind me, there was a muffled "Ow."

"I wonder where we are," I said. "Do you think we're under the street?"

"Nah," said Ellis. "We're probably all the way under the school by this time." Suddenly, he stopped. I jerked my candle back to avoid burning him. Behind me, there was another "Ow."

"Fork in the road," said Ellis. Sure enough, the main tunnel came to an abrupt end. Instead, there were two smaller tunnels, one going more or less straight, the other angling off to the right.

"Which way?" I asked.

"Straight, I think," said Ellis. For somebody who had been all through these tunnels, he sounded a little unsure. I glanced nervously at the narrow entrances. Which one of them was more likely to contain porcupines?

"Straight," announced Ellis. "Everybody put out the candles and use flashlights. We have to crawl."

"Wait," I said. "Everybody write your name on the ceiling with smoke." This took a while, since everybody decided to write more things, including insults.

Then we started crawling. This was worse than walking along all stooped over. For one thing, we were now in the trickle of water. For another, the flashlights were no good; it was almost impossible to see anything. I worried about broken glass, though I figured nobody would bother crawling this far up a drain just to break bottles. Then, up ahead, I saw a point of light. "Maybe that's a storm grate," I said. "We could get out that way."

The light was a long way off, and the drain was getting narrower. At this point, it was doubtful that any of us would be able to turn around. Roy Chapman Andrews never had to deal with anything like this, I thought. His problems usually involved bandits, camels, and getting stuck in the sand. Even Ellis was crawling a little slower than usual. Things couldn't possibly get any worse, I thought grimly.

Then, behind me, I heard Clay's voice for the first time that day.

"PORCUPINES!!!"

PUNCH BOWL

Sometime in late fall, I would review my finances. The Christmas I was in fourth grade, it turned out I had plenty of money for presents because of a lucrative sideline. Not only was I getting fifty cents per week allowance; I had also started getting fifty cents for each A and a quarter for each B on my report card. Add in the fact that Aunt Mary had sent me five dollars for my birthday back in May, and I was set to take the bus to H. L. Green's, where I did all my shopping.

It was easy to buy a Christmas present for Mama. You just got her English Lavender soap. I got her an umbrella once, but it didn't go over. I always got my father a tie. Green's had a limited selection, but the price was right. It was kind of hard to buy anything for Granny. I once got her some dusting powder, but she didn't know what it was and then Daddy got mad at her for not knowing what it was, so the next year I just got her an apron. This year I planned to get Ray a rubber alligator that moved when you squeezed a bulb. I thought it would make a nice addition to his rubber snake. Clay had started first grade and was having a lot of trouble with reading, so I rejected anything literary in favor of water colors. I got Patty Harris a Slinky. I wondered how many days it would be before Patty's mother Clara tried to hit Patty with a hammer. You could count on it every Christmas, sort of like *Amahl and the Night Visitors*. Though my holiday shopping experience was relatively stress-free, I realized that my parents were having their usual shopping problem.

Over the years Mama and Daddy had not had much luck with getting each other anything good for Christmas. Daddy had given Mama some nice jewelry, back when he was still married to Cammie, but apparently he wasn't putting as much effort into presents lately. Once he got Mama a fountain pen, and she retaliated by giving him a bathroom scale. Matters had finally reached the point where Daddy would just call up Montgomery Fair and tell whoever answered the phone to pick out some presents, wrap them up, and deliver them to the house. When Mama opened them, he was just as surprised as she was.

This year Daddy was doing most of his shopping by phone, because his doctor had told him to take it easy. It had been five years since his first heart attack, which had happened on Halloween, and the doctor had recently told him to have a couch installed in his office and lie down after lunch every day. Any time we wanted my father to play baseball or go swimming with us, he usually didn't because he said it was too much exercise for his heart. However, he didn't have any trouble screaming at us. This was strange, because you would think throwing a football would be a lot less exercise than throwing a chair. The doctor, who was really pretty lackadaisical, had shrugged when Daddy asked if he should be taking nitroglycerin. I was completely against him taking the stuff: what if he dropped the bottle?

Once school let out for the holidays, Ray and Clay and I settled into our Christmas routine, which consisted of watching *The Three Stooges* on TV all day long. We also went to Loveman's to see Santa Claus, who always terrified Clay.

On Christmas Eve, we followed our usual practice of driving around to see the Christmas decorations. The car radio was playing old Jack Benny programs. I had never heard anything but singing come out of a radio, but Daddy said, "This is the way radio used to be. They had all sorts of programs, not just singing." Jack Benny, who was currently wishing everyone a Merry Christmas and a happy 1947, was obviously a lot better than singing; I wondered what had gone wrong. By the time Edgar Bergen had also wished everybody a Merry Christmas, and Charlie McCarthy had reminded everybody to buy war bonds, we had arrived back at our driveway, nearly colliding with a big Montgomery Fair truck that was also pulling up. Two men wrestled a huge gift-wrapped box off the truck and rolled it up the steps to the porch. This, said my father excitedly, was Mama's Christmas present. I stared at the box, which was enormous.

I had no idea what it could be, since we already had a piano. The deliverymen hauled the box into the living room and put it next to the tree because it wouldn't fit under it. Mama paused to study the box whenever she passed through the living room. "I wonder what it could be?" she asked gaily. Really, I had no idea. It was big enough to be a complete new wardrobe. Maybe it was a marimba. We had all enjoyed seeing a couple of guys playing one on Ed Sullivan, but I doubted Mama had been impressed enough to want one. I didn't think the present was one of those vibrating fat-reducer belt machines like Myrtle Terry had either, and frankly I hoped it wasn't since Mama had gotten mad enough about the fountain pen. Maybe it was a saddle. Maybe we were going to get a horse. This was an alarming thought. Back in the fall, my father had said thoughtfully, "We should get a place in the country and move out of town. Y'all would have a great time playing if we lived on a farm." He had looked at the pile of files spilling off the dining room table before adding, "And besides, we need more room." I always enjoyed visiting my chicken at Libby's grandmother's house, so I was all for the idea, but that was the last I had heard of it. I had assumed that this was just another one of the things my father said from time to time, like "We should drive to California and go to Disneyland." Now I worried that my father had decided to go ahead and get a horse before we had a farm to keep it on. We'd have to put it in the garage. I tried to think of something more cheerful. Maybe it was an enormous jewelry box.

Christmas Day dawned bright and sunny, and we all raced into the living room to open our presents. I got an Etch A Sketch, some Barbie clothes, and a croquet set. Ray got an actual safe with some money in it and an electric train. Clay got a wagon and a cap pistol. Mama had gotten Daddy a paisley smoking jacket, which was attractive though not very practical since he had quit smoking except when the jury was out. Granny got an apron and a housecoat. She didn't say anything, so she apparently liked them.

By the time we got around to opening the mystery box, Lee and Libby had already arrived separately; we had gotten Lee an enormous sweater and Libby an umbrella which opened automatically. As soon as they left, Mama said, "Well! Let's see what this big box is!"

Beaming, she tore the paper off. Once the cardboard box was uncovered, we could all read the big letters. "Crystal punchbowl, 3 gallon capacity, with ladle and 36 cups. This side up."

"Punch bowl?" said my father. Apparently this was one of those presents that he hadn't selected personally. Mama just looked at him.

I thought Mama would open the box so we could see the punch bowl, but all she said was "Put it in there," gesturing toward the dining room. "We'll open it later." Then she started picking up paper off the floor.

We dragged the punch bowl box into the dining room and pushed it into the corner.

I passed it every time I went into the kitchen. Eventually, it started looking kind of permanent, and I stopped noticing that it was a box. Finally somebody put a stack of files on it. Really, it was sort of handy, almost like a table.

ROLE MODEL

My father died one January night while I was in fourth grade. In fact, he died during *The Many Loves of Dobie Gillis*, though that didn't have anything to do with it. By the time my father figured out that what he had wasn't indigestion, we couldn't get in touch with the doctor who, it later turned out, had been drunk in a bowling alley. There was some talk of my mother going for help, but she didn't know how to back the car down the driveway. We tried calling the ambulance, but their line was busy.

We got more than four hundred sympathy notes, which my mother put in the bottom drawer of the secretary, on top of the newspaper with the headline "Nazis Quit."

Ray and Clay and I stayed out of school for a week. My godmother, Miss Bonnie Terrell, urged me to go back. "It won't get any easier," she said.

She was right. My main problem was kids telling me they were sorry. This always made me mad, though I wasn't sure why. I would usually say something like "Well, it wasn't your fault."

The week after the funeral, I heard my mother on the phone with Miss Bonnie. "Grocery store," she said, and then "there's no way around it." People had brought us a lot of food, including something called a Tunnel of Fudge Cake, which was great, but we had pretty much eaten it all. My mother hung up the phone and sighed. My parents had always gone to the store together. My father would push the cart and tell my mother what to get. "Come on," said my mother. "I need you to help me back the car down the driveway."

I stood by the corner of the house and warned my mother when she was getting too close. It took her about ten minutes to get the car down to the street. I thought I'd have time to watch television, but she was back in fifteen minutes, carrying a big bag of groceries. She looked a little bewildered. "There was nothing to it," she said. "I just bought whatever I wanted and paid the girl."

After my father died, my mother started sitting in the big green chair, the one with the ottoman, rather than the little rocking chair—which, now that I looked at it, didn't seem all that comfortable. My mother and Granny stopped speaking to each other, which was a relief, except that I had to carry messages between them. Finally my mother said we would have to economize. I immediately offered to quit piano lessons, but it turned out that wasn't what she meant. We all started packing our lunches, which was good since there was an ongoing rumor that the lunchroom was serving us war-surplus horsemeat.

One day I went into what had been my parents' bedroom to find Mama staring at the ceiling, which had a large crack running through it. "We're going to have to paint," she said. "I don't see," she continued, "why we can't just paint it ourselves." I wasn't sure. I had seen people paint on television, but they were the Three Stooges.

There turned out to be more than met the eye to painting the ceiling. For one thing, it was cracked, meaning that we had to plaster. "You just mix this stuff up," said my mother confidently, "and then smear it on the crack." She put a Baggie over her hair, climbed up on the ladder which Ray, Clay, and I held, and slapped the plaster over the crack. A lot of it fell on the floor. Finally she got most of it to stick, after which we just had to wait for it to dry before painting over it. This part was actually fun. We had a roller with a long handle on it and we took turns splattering the paint on the ceiling.

The next day, all the paint covering the crack fell off.

"Huh," said my mother. She put an extra thick coat of paint right over the crack.

The next day, it fell off again. "This is ridiculous," said my mother. After she got off the phone with the paint store, she muttered, "Denatured alcohol. Why didn't they say so?"

After she got back on the ladder and coated the plaster with denatured alcohol, we painted the ceiling for what turned out to be the last time.

I thought we were doing pretty well. My mother and Granny had resumed speaking, which wasn't good, but things were generally peaceful. We should have had less income but it turned out that since my mother didn't bet on anything we had enough money as long as we kept packing lunches.

Mama, though, was worried. I heard her on the phone to Miss Bonnie. "A man's influence," she was saying. "Someone they can look up to. Especially the boys." Apparently, my mother was having trouble thinking of a man who could be a good influence on us. Ellis Chalmers's father was the obvious candidate, since the Chalmerses had plenty of money and Mrs. Chalmers's grandmother had once danced with Jefferson Davis, but about this time Mr. Chalmers got beat up late one night at Sully's Barbecue by a man who, according to the police report, didn't like his hat.

Then, Miss Bonnie suggested that Don, her husband, would be a good role model and invited us all to come to her daughter Lana's birthday party so Ray and Clay could spend some time with Don.

Lana was Ray's age, and I didn't usually play with her because I was scared of her. She was built like a fireplug, had belligerent red hair, and liked to jump on people. When we got to the Terrells' ranch-style house, Lana was running through the little front yard chasing a group of kids with a baseball bat. I immediately stood behind Ray. "Bum bum bum!" screamed Lana; "Here I come!!" The front of her frilly yellow dress had a smear of ketchup, unless it was blood.

"Lana!" yelled Miss Bonnie. Lana screeched reluctantly to a halt. "You take Kathie, Ray, and Clay around back and play catch with your father."

Lana looked doubtful. "If you say so," she said. "Come on."

Miss Bonnie should have been in a good mood. She was all dressed up, in a purple dress that didn't really go with her hair and high-heel shoes—and her own birthday had been one day earlier. Apparently, though, something had gone wrong. As she and my mother went in the house, she was muttering, "Not one thing. He could have gotten me a card."

We went in the backyard where Don, looking flushed, was leaning on the car. "Let's play catch," said Lana. "I got a new mitt for my birthday." Don smiled broadly at Ray and Clay. Lana beat her baseball bat on the ground. "Right over the plate!" she yelled. Ray and Clay looked scared. I went in the house.

Mrs. Wilton, Miss Bonnie's mother, was pouring Cokes for my mother and Miss Bonnie. "Never takes her nowhere," she was saying. Mrs. Wilton lived with the Terrells. It was sort of like Granny living with us, except Mrs. Wilton didn't dip snuff.

I wandered in the TV room. The Terrells had a separate room just for watching their color television. Unfortunately, a commercial was showing, so I went back in the kitchen. There on the table, sitting on a tray, was a doll with a big fluffy yellow skirt—but then I realized that though the doll was real, the skirt was a dome-shaped cake with swirls of ruffled yellow icing. "Wow," I said. A couple of other kids who apparently weren't baseball fans had come in. "Wow," they said. One of them reached out a tentative hand.

Miss Bonnie snatched the cake up. The cake wasn't for us to eat, she said, putting it in a cabinet. We were going to have cupcakes. She opened a box, revealing a pile of little cakes with plain white icing. At this point, Ray and Clay came in, followed by Lana with her baseball bat. "Where is your father?" asked Miss Bonnie, her eyes narrowed. Lana shrugged. "He said he had to go do something," she said. "Let's play tag!" she yelled, swinging her bat. I ducked.

Finally Lana's father came in, smiling and walking a little unsteadily. He held out a box. "Belated birthday," he said happily to Miss Bonnie. She opened the box. There was a big purple orchid corsage. "A real orchid," I said. Mrs. Wilton peered into the box. "I don't know where the hell you're going to wear that," she said.

"Well," said my mother brightly, "we'd better go." "I had a nice time," I added, thinking that I hadn't even gotten a cupcake.

"You need any help backing the car out?" asked Don, who was now leaning on the kitchen counter.

"No, no, that's all right," said my mother, shooing us ahead of her. "We can manage."

We got in the car. "Mrs. Wilton said 'hell,'" I said.

"No she didn't," said my mother firmly. "She said 'I don't know where in the world you're going to wear it.'"

I looked out the window.

She'd said hell.

MISSISSIPPI

We had been to Mississippi a few times since Aunt Katherine died, but it wasn't the same. For one thing, Uncle Jule had gotten drunk one night and accidentally set fire to the house by throwing a bottle that he mistakenly assumed was empty into a gas heater. After Uncle Jule died, a couple of months after my father, we went to Mississippi to get whatever hadn't burned up so Mama could sell the house to Emil Dennis, who owned the only store in Ovett.

Emil had grown up with Mama. Apparently something awful had happened in Syria during the early 1920s and that was how Emil's family had ended up in the middle of nowhere. The rest of the people in Ovett were pretty hostile to the Syrians, whom they called Dagoes— probably feeling that they had to call them something—but Mama and her family got along with them. After all, they had something in common, since the rest of the people in Ovett were also hostile to Mama's family for being Presbyterians.

Aunt Katherine's house was pretty much unrecognizable, except for the big gardenia bush out front, which was in full bloom. The steps were sagging, there was a big tree limb on the roof, and the screen door was off its hinges. Inside, things were worse. The whole place smelled sort of scorched. I retrieved the pink ceramic flamingo that I had given Aunt Katherine off the piano, which was missing half its keys. Mama recovered a quilt, a couple of framed photographs, and some books, but everything else in the house was pretty much broken, burned up, or missing. As we looked around, we heard a weird humming noise in the direction of the kitchen. It turned out to be coming from thousands of bees that had moved in after Uncle Jule died. We left the house pretty abruptly at that point and walked around the yard, but the chicken house had fallen down along with the fence; there wasn't much to see, so we got back in the car. As we drove off, Mama glanced in the rear view mirror at her former home. "So much for that," she said. Mama cheered up a little, though, as we rounded a bend in the dirt road, because we were headed for my Great-aunt Mary's house, near the bigger town of Laurel. Since Aunt Mary and Uncle Oree lived right next door to their daughter Frances and her husband Donald, we'd also be visiting them and their children, Bonnie and David. "Those children," said Mama happily, "have such a wonderful place to play and grow up. I just wish we could live out in the country." While she talked, we drove down winding roads into the pine trees, further and further from civilization. Aunt Mary and Uncle Oree lived in a little house covered with a sort of gritty siding that was supposed to look like bricks but didn't. The house was surrounded by acres of farmland; they grew most of their own food and had once owned a mule, but he had died, and apparently there was a mule shortage, since they hadn't replaced him. They still had chickens, though, and plenty of cats. As we walked up the dirt driveway to the house, a few of them were winding around on the little porch, which was not as nice as Aunt Katherine's because it wasn't screened. Aunt Mary was tiny and white-haired. Uncle Oree, a big shy man, did most of the cooking and housework; Aunt Mary's contribution was to take care of the garden and bake bread for the cats. When Aunt Mary was young her family had lived in a big fine house and considered themselves to be a higher social class than the other people in Ovett. Admittedly, the bar was set pretty low. Since there was nobody suitable for her to marry, the family had decided that Aunt Mary should be an old maid schoolteacher like Aunt Katherine. However, Aunt Mary thought that was a bad idea, so she climbed out the window and married Uncle Oree, who Mama described as a dirt farmer. I wasn't sure what this meant. I thought all farms had dirt.

Aunt Mary and Uncle Oree were glad to see us. Aunt Mary showed me her flower garden, which was full of old-fashioned flowers like sweet peas, verbena, and some big plumy purple things she called prince's-feathers. I was all in favor of spending the whole day at Aunt

Mary's getting to know some of her fifteen cats, but pretty soon every-body decided we should go next door to Frances and Donald's farm. You could hear their chickens—thousands of them—as we pulled up in the driveway. The chickens lived in big plastic-covered houses in back of the little farmhouse. I was fascinated. I had never seen chicken farming on such a grand scale. I went around the houses with David, who explained how they got the food and water to the chickens, which he called "broilers." His cat, Pat the Cat, followed us. It was Pat's practice, according to David, to lurk outside the chicken house waiting for a chicken to peer out from between the slats, at which Pat would bite off its head. While I thought this story was interesting if true, I suspected David of making things up. Earlier, when Ray, Clay, and I had been walking around Aunt Mary's house with him, David had pointed to an old pump which stood beneath a catalpa tree. He claimed that all you had to do was pump the handle, and catalpa worms, suitable for fish bait, would pour forth. We tried it a couple of times, but he said we weren't pumping hard enough.

Now, as we walked around, I decided that I wouldn't believe the story about Pat unless I saw him biting off heads. Back of the chicken house, Ray and Clay spotted a small pond in the middle of a pasture which also contained a number of cows, but David dissuaded them from exploring it, saying the pasture was infested with pythons.

We went back in the house. Aunt Mary had apparently been dis-cussing some of our relatives I hadn't met. "None of the MacDonalds," she was saying, "ever got much out of life. All the MacDonalds were sad." I wondered briefly who the MacDonalds were, then decided that I was just as well off without knowing. I wandered back in the kitchen and sat down at the table, which was covered with a plastic tablecloth. David asked if I wanted some water. What I really wanted was a Coke, but apparently they didn't have any. The water, which came from a well, tasted funny. Maybe it was time for lunch, I thought, brightening up. Aunt Mary, like Aunt Katherine, made terrific cakes. "What time is it?" I asked, glancing around for a clock. David shrugged. "Who knows?" he said, adding "Our clock broke."

I was appalled. "Well, does anybody have a watch?" "Nope." "Well, how do you ever know what time it is?" David thought. "I guess we could call the Time and Temperature number." We called the Time and Temperature number from a black wall phone. "Bank at First Southern," said a mechanical voice. "Where your money works overtime. Local time is 11:31." We hung up before we heard the temperature.

At least it was close to lunchtime. We walked back through the field to Aunt Mary's house, Mama and Aunt Mary following in the car. In the kitchen, Uncle Oree was frying chicken and talking to four cats who were sitting hopefully around his feet. I was a little alarmed. We'd seen an awful lot of chickens that morning, and I wasn't sure that one of them hadn't wound up dead. A big gray-striped cat ended up sitting under my chair and I gave some of my chicken to him. At least one part of lunch was a hit; dessert was coconut cake with fresh strawberries from Aunt Mary's garden.

After lunch we walked back down to Frances's house. It seemed to me that walking back and forth took up most of people's day around here. I was still trying to figure out how life in the country really worked. "How do you get to school?" I asked David. "Take the bus, of course," he said, adding, "Look out, that's a cow pie!" to Ray, who was examining something on the ground. David, I reflected, was becoming a pathological liar, though the part about the bus sort of made sense. We hadn't driven past anything that remotely resembled a school, so he sure couldn't walk. "How," I asked, "do you know when to catch the bus?" David gave me a look. "It's summer," he pointed out. "By fall, we'll have gotten the clock fixed. Probably." At this point, our walk took us under pine trees. From the top of one, a mockingbird was singing away. The country was pretty, but I was still having trouble adjusting. As soon as we got back inside Frances's house, I asked, "What time is it now?"

Eventually, David and Bonnie got summoned to do chores, and Ray and Clay and I fled back to Aunt Mary's. On the way, I crawled into our car to see the dashboard clock. Four-twelve P.M.

The porch was the coolest spot around Aunt Mary's. I climbed into the swing with the gray cat and tried to read one of the books we had gotten from Aunt Katherine's house. *Mrs. Mike* was about a young woman who marries a Canadian Mountie and moves to the Canadian wilderness. Things started going wrong almost at once, and by the time I gave up and put the book in the trash pile, a person had been

70

eaten by a bear, two more people had burned up in a forest fire, and a bunch of children had died from diphtheria. I shuddered. Apparently the country got worse and worse the farther out in it you went, until you hit the Canadian wilderness and all hell broke loose.

I brooded on this insight as we got in the car to leave, Aunt Mary handing me an envelope full of prince's-feather seeds as an early birthday present. "That's right," said Mama cheerfully, waving out the open window as we jolted back down the dirt driveway. "You've got a birthday coming up. What do you want for your present?"

"A watch," I said.

MOSS POINT

Mr. and Mrs. Nolte were not our friends. That's what Mama always said whenever Ellie Nolte called to invite herself to stay with us while she researched her ancestors at the state archives. "They were his friends, not mine," Mama would mutter as she rooted through the linen closet, trying to find spare sheets that did not have rips in them. When the Noltes asked us to go to their house at Moss Point for vacation the summer after my father died, I wrote Great-aunt Mary, "We are going to Moss Point with our acquaintances, the Noltes."

It was accurate, but I had to admit it looked a little formal.

Moss Point was on a bayou not far from Mobile. I looked up "bayou," and it said "a small bay," which was no help. I had heard of people having beach houses, though unfortunately no one we knew, but wasn't sure why you'd go to the trouble of having a house on a small bay.

I had the feeling that we were going to a house in a swamp, so I packed a bunch of *National Geographics* in case I got bored. Moss Point itself was a little bitty town in Mississippi, but the Noltes' house was outside of town up a dirt track that wound among the pine trees. We thought we were lost, but finally we spotted the Noltes' new Buick parked in front of a big unpainted two-story house. The house didn't look very promising from the outside, but inside was a different story. It was big and shadowy and had huge rooms with built-in bookcases and big squashy sofas and chairs. From the screened back porch, you could see a boathouse and pier and the bayou, which looked to me more like a big lake. Dan Nolte seemed especially glad to see Mama. He hugged her enthusiastically, called her "dear Virginia," and picked up her suitcase, which he put down when Ellie Nolte glared at him. Meanwhile, I discovered a surprise—a door which opened to reveal a stairway to the second floor. I wasn't sure why anybody would build a door across the bottom of their stairs. If it was to keep hot air out, it hadn't worked. Nevertheless, I was impressed when I reached the top of the stairs to find an enormous room lined with beds. This, said Timmy Nolte, who, with his sister Helen, had sort of materialized, was where all the kids would sleep. This struck me as a great idea.

After we put our suitcases in the sleeping room, we all ran down to the boathouse, where I was alarmed to see King, Timmy's enormous German Shepherd. He looked like something Adolf Hitler would have as a pet. Even though Timmy kept saying, "He won't bite," and even though I couldn't imagine Timmy getting within a hundred yards of a dangerous animal, I kept my distance from the huge dog, who ignored me in favor of barking at a crab. The water was shallow; when I walked out onto the little pier, I could see plenty of crabs swimming past or crawling around the bottom. "Can we go crabbing?" I asked excitedly. "Yeah," said Timmy. "Just watch out and don't let any of them pinch you."

Crabbing would have to wait, though, because, according to Ellie, after supper we were going to have a visitor: Captain Billy, a neighbor who had his own museum. He was, she said, looking directly at my mother, a widower.

I had never met anybody who owned a whole museum and was prepared to be impressed, but Captain Billy turned out to be a scrawny little man who smoked Lucky Strikes and didn't have all his teeth. He looked like he belonged in jail. At one point he pulled out a *Mad* magazine that he apparently carried with him at all times, flipped through it, and read aloud from a fake ad for a "Mayjag" washer. Judging by the illustration, a family of hillbillies had gotten a washer and turned it into a still. They were all gathered around the machine, holding jugs. The caption read "After fifteen years, our May-jag is a workin' still!"

"See?" said Captain Billy, holding the magazine under Mama's nose. "It says 'Our Mayjag is a workin' still!' Haw haw haw!"

"Ha," said Mama weakly, moving her chair back.

Before Captain Billy could get around to reading us "Spy versus Spy," Ellie stood up. We were all, she beamed, going to visit Captain Billy's Museum. Led by Captain Billy, we trooped down the dirt road to a building that looked like a cross between a garage and a haunted shack. A tree was leaning on the roof. Painted on what looked like it used to be a door was a faded sign announcing "Captain Billy's Museum of the Sea."

The Museum of the Sea turned out to be two or three hundred shark jaws, some of them enormous. Ray and Clay were awestruck. I was impressed by some of the bigger jaws, but I didn't see how this amounted to a Museum of the Sea. If he'd said Museum of the Shark I might have felt differently.

Timmy and Helen had undoubtedly seen the Museum of the Sea before; Timmy maintained a respectful distance from the shark teeth, and Helen, eating a donut, stared off into space. "Want to go crabbing tomorrow?" I asked Timmy. "Sure," he said, "if there aren't too many mosquitoes."

He wasn't kidding about the mosquitoes. Clouds of them pursued us all the way back to the Noltes' house. Before we filed upstairs to bed, we all sprayed ourselves with Off.

I was kind of hoping Captain Billy wouldn't become a permanent fixture, and sure enough, we didn't see him or his *Mad* magazine any more. Possibly Mama had said something discouraging to Ellie. At any rate, by the following morning things were back to normal. Dan resumed reading the newspaper and not talking, and Ellie resumed telling us about how she was related to Marie Antoinette, whom she called "Cuz Marie." Dan occasionally gave Mama a sad glance from behind the paper, but I didn't have much time to worry about it because, bright and early, we went crabbing.

The first step in crabbing was to find a dead fish. This was easy; we just walked along the edge of the water. Timmy, who was using a paper towel to pick up the fish, instructed us to tie the fish to a string, which we then threw overboard from the pier. When a crab came to inspect the fish, we gently pulled in the string, then slid a net under the crab and pulled it in, dumping it into a deep peach basket lined with wet Spanish moss. Crabbing was tricky; many a crab managed to get away. Just as I got my net under a promising crab, King fell in. Following his usual practice of barking at crabs, he had leaned over too far. Timmy was horrified, even though the water was only two feet deep, and King, looking vaguely embarrassed, had merely walked to shore. "He'll get water in his ears! He'll get water in his ears!" wailed Timmy, hauling the bewildered King off to the house. I thought it was actually more significant that King and Timmy, working together, had undoubtedly scared off every crab between Moss Point and Pascagoula.

Peering intently into the water, I worked my way around to the farthest point of the pier, and it was here that I ran into the wasp nest. Three of them nailed me before I was able to vault onto dry land and run for the house, followed immediately by Ray and Clay. We sped past Helen, who was lying in a hammock, and Timmy, who was drying King with a fluffy towel.

I wasn't allergic to wasps, but I didn't feel all that good. Mama wondered if I ought to go to a doctor, but it turned out there wasn't one. Ellie produced a small bottle of ammonia from her purse, saying that she kept it around at all times in case of faintness, and I spent most of the afternoon lying on the couch, dabbing ammonia on the stings. I couldn't tell if this was doing any good, but by the time Ray and Clay appeared, yelling that we were going to clean the crabs, I got up and made my way to the porch.

Cleaning the crabs turned out to be pretty violent. First we pulled their claws and legs off, then we got a knife and opened up the flap they had on their undersides, sort of like opening an envelope. Then we got rid of what Timmy called "dead man's fingers" which I think were actually their lungs.

After we cleaned the crabs, Dan set fire to the wasps' nest. Ray and Clay watched, enthralled; Timmy went into the house, and Helen ate an Oreo.

Ellie fried the crabs for dinner. I wasn't sure how to describe what we were eating. I didn't want to tell people I had eaten fried crab bodies, even though it was accurate. Ellie said they were called "crab middles."

On our last morning in Moss Point, we went out in the rowboat. Once we rounded the little point of land that the Noltes' house was on, I could see the bayou stretching away in all directions. High grass covered the banks, and cypresses grew out of the water. Dan pointed out a mud track down the bank that he called an alligator slide, but I figured that since Timmy had been willing to get into the boat, there weren't really any alligators.

As I packed to go home, I glanced out the window to the boathouse and pier, one board of which was charred where Dan had set fire to the wasps. Moss Point wasn't perfect—in addition to wasps, it had Captain Billy. But, I thought as I packed the *National Geographics* I hadn't even opened, Moss Point would go down in history. It was the first place I'd ever been that was better than I had imagined.

AUDUBON CLUB

In fifth grade, I got the worst teacher I had ever had, which was saying something. Except for her hair, which she apparently colored with iodine, Miss Rolla looked almost exactly like the guy who starred on *Highway Patrol*. That wasn't the problem, especially since *Highway Patrol* was a good show.

The bad thing about Miss Rolla was that she had so many rules, and she usually didn't tell you about them until after you'd broken one. You had to call her "ma'am," which wasn't unusual, though I never remembered to do it, and you weren't allowed to chew gum, which went without saying. Then there were the other rules. You were not allowed to write with anything other than a #2 pencil. You were not allowed to look at the clock. You were not allowed to look out the window. If you dropped something, you were not allowed to bend over to pick it up without raising your hand to ask for permission.

It was impossible for one person to enforce all those rules, especially the one about looking at the clock, which is why Miss Rolla appointed classroom monitors. The main qualification for being a classroom monitor was willingness to tattle, but having a mean nature also came in handy. This was why Wally Gold, runner-up for meanest boy in school, was the head monitor. He was not above poking you until you turned around and told him to drop dead, after which he would tell on you for turning around.

I was out sick as much as humanly possible.

The problem wasn't so much my physical health, but my nerves, which were shot. Even at home, I caught myself raising my hand to get permission to go to the bathroom.

My mother was tired of hearing me complain. "She can't possibly be as bad as that," she said. "Why don't you try to find something nice about her?"

Fat chance.

I thought to myself that Miss Rolla was enough to drive anybody crazy, and eventually I almost got confirmation of my theory. One morning Miss Rolla fixed me with what looked like a smile. "Have you heard," she asked, "about Celia Bronson?"

"Yeah," I said, belatedly adding "ma'am." Everybody had heard about Celia Bronson. Her bright yellow hair, long red fingernails, and fishnet stockings attracted plenty of notice, and just the other day she had fallen out of a car into the front yard of the house she shared with her parents and the small boy who was popularly referred to as her brother. By this time, people had also heard that during her latest visit to Tuscaloosa, Celia had been a patient at Bryce Hospital.

"She's dead," continued Miss Rolla silkily. "Someone she met in the insane asylum ran over her with his car."

I was shocked. I was also wondering if it was the same car.

"I could see it coming. She was in this class," said Miss Rolla, looking nostalgic. "Even then, she behaved oddly. She always dusted off her chair before she sat in it." Some of the Yankee kids, especially the ones who sat near the open window where the seats were always dirty, shifted uncomfortably.

"I have an announcement," continued Miss Rolla, dismissing Celia with a wave of her hand. "We are going to start a chapter of Junior Audubon in this class. We will meet each Friday from 2:30 to 2:50. You will each be assigned to do a report upon a bird."

I perked up. Birds! I already knew about Audubon—we had a book called *Audubon's Birds of America* with paintings of hundreds of birds, my favorite of which was the flamingo.

In my excitement, I almost forgot about Celia being run over, but by the time I got home I had remembered to feel sad. I expected to find the entire block descending on the Bronsons' house with food, the way they'd besieged us when my father died, but nothing was happening. The Bronsons' house was dark; my mother said they'd gone out of town. "Poor Celia," said my mother.

I decided to cheer her up. "Guess what? We're going to have a Junior Audubon club at school."

"Well!" said my mother brightly. "That will give you a little something to look forward to."

It also gave me something to work on. My flamingo report, I decided, would break new ground. The first thing I needed was a color illustration. I would have to draw a flamingo. After several false starts, I came out with a completely recognizable likeness on poster board, colored with crayons. The following Friday, I confidently dragged my visual aid and my five-page report into class.

Before Junior Audubon, we were going to have a report from Tommy Arnold on his extra-credit science project. The science fair was coming up, and supposedly the best project from each room would be entered in the fair, but I didn't see how this was going to happen, since Miss Rolla never liked anybody's project.

Tommy stood up, carrying a box. Evidently, he thought he had a chance; as he opened the box, he was looking pleased with himself. "This," he said, "is a sweet potato, and this is a battery. So all I do is hook up the battery to the sweet potato and"—there was a pause while he struggled with the battery—"here we have a sweet potato clock!"

I was pretty impressed and could see all sorts of practical applications for the technology, but Miss Rolla was frowning. "Tommy," she said softly, "if you expect to receive extra credit for a science project, you must develop something which will benefit the class as a whole. This classroom already has a clock." At this, several kids automatically turned to look at the clock. I could see Wally Gold making notes.

I didn't know how Tommy could be expected to benefit a whole roomful of people from a potato, and apparently neither did he. He took his seat behind me, muttering, "She's trying to destroy my interest in science." I didn't think he needed to worry. His interest in science was probably as indestructible as my interest in birds.

Was it time for Junior Audubon yet?

"You looked at the clock," said Wally Gold.

"Shut up, Goldfinch," I said, fairly pleased at having coined a bird-related insult.

"Before we begin," said Miss Rolla, "a few ground rules. Anyone who talks, looks at the clock, turns around, bends over, or otherwise violates one of our classroom rules will be fined ten cents."

Wally Gold looked overjoyed, even though he probably wasn't going to get to keep the money.

First up was Robin Godwin, who reported on robins. Not very imaginative. As she sat down to polite applause, I waved my hand frantically to go next, knocking my poster to the floor in the process. "Oops," I said, bending down to grab it. Miss Rolla frowned, but waved for me to proceed.

I cleared my throat. What followed may have been the most complete flamingo report ever made to a fifth-grade class. I touched on diet, feeding method and lifestyle, noting that the feeding call was "eep." I finished by pointing to my illustration, calling the class's attention to the fact that, since the flamingo feeds with its head upside-down, its downward-hooked bill makes it appear to be smiling. I waited for the applause. Miss Rolla cleared her throat.

"Ten cents, please," she said.

"Huh?" I said. "Ma'am."

"You leaned over. Ten cents please."

"Oh. Well, I dropped my—"

"Ten cents, please." At that point, the bell rang.

Just outside the school door was a blue jay. I barely glanced at it. It was possible, I thought gloomily, to destroy a person's interest in birds, if you worked at it. Then, around the corner of the cafeteria, I saw something which surprised me. It was Tommy Arnold, crouched by a Pontiac. "What's going on?" I asked.

"Shhh!" hissed Tommy. "Don't tell."

"Okay," I said. "What is it?"

Tommy reached back into his science-project box. "This," he said, holding it up, "is a sweet potato, and THIS"—he waved an arm at the Pontiac—"is Rolla's car. So all I do is"—here he bent over behind the car—"jam this potato up the tailpipe"—he straightened up, dusting his hands—"and when she cranks it up, Pow! The old nut asphyxiates!"

"Ah," I said. Tommy really knew his science.

Swinging my book bag, I sauntered away. Down at the corner, the Popsicle boy was just getting ready to close up shop. "Hey!" I yelled. "Wait up!"

I passed the Bronsons' house, walking slowly so as not to get my raspberry Popsicle all over me.

There was a car in the drive, but the shades were still pulled. "Celia," I thought, "if you can hear me, be sure and read tomorrow's newspaper."

As I started up my own driveway, I paused. There on the holly bush were dozens of birds. Little crested birds, with a characteristic red patch on their wings, enthusiastically eating the holly berries.

"Cedar waxwing," I said.

PIANO

Mama's Aunt Katherine taught piano and was deadly serious about it. At one time, Mama had been serious about music too—when she and my father got married, he bought her a piano, explaining that she already had her late mother's engagement ring. I didn't see why he couldn't have bought her a ring anyway. Eventually, Mama stopped playing the piano except for Sunday school, but she was determined that I take lessons. Apparently there was some sort of piano piece by Rachmaninoff that was so difficult that anyone who learned it went crazy. When I started piano lessons in first grade, Mama had said solemnly that, although she had never been able to learn this piece, she wanted me to learn it. I didn't think this sounded like a good idea.

Anybody who took piano at Cloverdale School got to get out of classes early. This powerful inducement made up for the smallness of the piano room, which had been a closet. It was just large enough for an upright piano and an old lady. These piano teachers were a mixed bag, and you never knew who you were going to get. I went from a fairly easygoing old lady who said I had great flexibility to a crazy old bat who took it personally every time I hit a wrong note. "No, no, no, dahling!" she would moan, laying her head on the piano in what I thought was an overly dramatic manner. She appeared to think I was doing it on purpose.

Aside from the annoying teacher, the worst thing about taking piano was having to practice. Every time I turned around, I was either practicing piano or being nagged by Mama about practicing. Apparently Aunt Katherine had made her practice at least two hours a day. I didn't think Rachmaninoff himself had had to practice that much.

That was another thing. As the years went by, it seemed to me that not only was I never going to get a chance to memorize the Rachmaninoff piece that made you go insane; I was also probably never going to get much beyond "Twinkle, Twinkle, Little Star."

My father's main contribution to my musical studies was to yell "I don't hear any practicing going on," if I happened to be sitting on the piano bench thinking about something.

After my father died, I offered to quit piano, just in case we could no longer afford it, but my offer wasn't accepted. Taking piano didn't qualify as a financial hardship, since it was only twenty-five cents a lesson. The sheet music, which we were supposed to buy from the piano teacher, was also reasonably priced at twenty-five cents. It was also possible to buy used music for a dime, and even to borrow music for free if the teacher was one of the less crazy ones.

Though taking piano was not a burden financially, it was sort of hard on my nerves. Once we were watching an episode of Ed Sullivan featuring a little Chinese girl who was a genius at playing the piano. The piece she was playing wasn't the Rachmaninoff thing, but it sounded pretty complicated, and at the end Ed Sullivan was congratulating the kid. As a joke, she said "American kids just don't practice enough!"—at which Mama pointed at me. I didn't think this was particularly fair.

From time to time, the issue of me quitting piano came up, but never in a straightforward fashion. Usually, I would be practicing in a desultory manner, hitting wrong notes fairly frequently, and saying that I wanted to go outside. At this point, Mama would sigh tragically and say, "Well if that's the way you feel, I guess you might just as well go ahead and quit taking piano." I would promptly say, "Oh no, I want to take piano," which was ridiculous since I didn't.

One good thing about taking piano was the annual piano competition which took place at Haverty's Music Store downtown, in their piano salesroom. There I would perch at one of the pianos, in front of a small but select audience of judges who had probably been imported from Birmingham or somewhere else known for its musical sophistication. I would calmly announce the name of my piece, usually something with an unimaginative title like "Spinning Song," dazzle them with my technique, and, if all went well, win a coveted certificate of excellence. Then we would go eat lunch.

In the spring of fifth grade, my eyes started going bad. I couldn't see the board. It wasn't that I couldn't see what was written on the board, I couldn't see that there was a board. This was a problem, because I was trying to avoid Miss Rolla, and sitting in the front row was the equivalent of having a target painted on you. I finally mentioned something to Mama, who had 20/20 eyesight, about it. A trip to the eye doctor revealed that I now had 20/400 vision and would have to wear glasses. I had halfway expected Mama to say something cheerful like "Well! Now you'll be able to see!" Instead, she just seemed sad and disappointed. I thought I knew what was going on. Mama had scrapbooks that she had been keeping since she was little. Usually these scrapbooks were literally scraps, pasted into an old ledger from her father's general store, but starting at about the time she turned twelve, the scrapbooks began including newspaper articles about her winning one beauty pageant after another, along with ads for plays in which she'd appeared and invitations to dances. All this was in addition to programs from piano recitals in which she'd starred. Obviously, now that I had to wear glasses I could forget following in her footsteps as far as the beauty pageants and dances were concerned. Though I might get to appear in a play if it had a part for a librarian, I realized that piano was now my only real chance to become a social success.

I should practice more, I thought grimly. For the spring recital, I was finally going to play something people had heard of—*Moonlight Sonata*. As the weather warmed up, I dutifully tinkled away at the piano, motivated partly by my foolproof plan: in addition to my boffo performance, I would wow the judges with the sophistication of my outfit.

Knee socks.

I was getting tired of showing up in socks folded down to the ankle. Knee socks were obviously more of a fashion statement and would go some way toward making up for the glasses. Thus it was that, on a spring Saturday, I felt pretty pleased with myself as we rolled up at Haverty's. I had on a black-and-white checked dress with matching hairband, the whole ensemble set off by the dazzling white knee socks and black patent shoes. The only cloud on my musical horizon was my suspicion that I ought to have practiced more, since the judges probably had some idea of how *Moonlight Sonata* was supposed to sound. Mama settled herself in the second row, right behind the judges.

"I'm going to go in the back room and practice a little," I said.

She beamed approvingly.

The back room, where Haverty's stored their excess pianos, was traditionally where piano students waited for their turn to perform. There was one kid already there, but she wasn't practicing. Instead, she was sitting on a piano stool, making it go around and around. This kid had on a fluffy pink dress which didn't really go with her chopped-off mousy brown hair and missing front tooth. "Hey," she said. "My name's Libby. You want to go up in the attic?" I didn't even know Haverty's had an attic. Libby pointed at a stairway which was nearly hidden by a large pile of dusty boxes.

"No," I said, adding belatedly, "My name's Kathie. I'm going to practice."

Libby stopped in mid-spin to give me a suspicious look. "What for?"

I was confused. "Well, so I can get a certificate of excellence," I said, politely refraining from adding "you moron."

Libby gave a fairly nasty laugh and resumed spinning. "Aw, my dad told me those certificates of excellence are a fraud. They only give them out to kids who buy the most sheet music."

At this point, I had several thoughts, in no particular order:

One: Who, exactly, did Libby's father think he was?

Two: How did the judges know how much sheet music you bought, and did you only get half credit if you bought it used?

Three: How many certificates of excellence had Libby personally gotten?

Although I was pretty sure Libby's father was lying like a dog, the exchange rankled. I cast a doubtful look at my own twenty-five-cent sheet music.

"Come on!" yelled Libby, heading straight for the stairs. "The attic's great! I went up there last year! They've got old trunks and everything!"

I was torn.

"Come on!" yelled Libby again, more insistently. "I'm telling you it's fun!"

I shrugged and followed her up the stairs.

The attic was not all that much fun. There was nothing in the old trunks, and you had to climb over a lot of dusty boxes to get at them. About the time I came back downstairs, I was beginning to think crawling around the attic might not have been a good idea.

I glanced down at my formerly white socks. Covered with dust from the ankle up. Libby was covered with dust, too, not that it was much consolation. She wasn't even trying for a certificate of excellence. As I grimly rolled my socks down to cover the damage, I wondered exactly how long I was going to go around doing things I didn't want to do, just because somebody thought I should.

I got another certificate of excellence.

The next time Mama, sighing deeply, said, "Well, maybe you'd just better stop taking piano," I said, "Okay."

1963

Although things went downhill in a hurry, 1963 had actually started on a hopeful note. One day in February, Mama came back from the beauty parlor with her hair in a French twist. She was carrying a library book titled *Teach Yourself Bridge*. "I may take bridge lessons," she said cheerfully. "I could sign up at the Y. Mary

Lyles plays bridge with some ladies every other Saturday, and I may start going."

Mary Lyles was Mama's friend from before she got married. A thin, sad-looking lady, she had come to the house after my father died, bringing us a jar of red cinnamon apple rings. She had big dark circles under her eyes. I didn't know if this was because she felt sorry for us or just because she smoked one cigarette after another, completely filling our biggest ashtray.

Mama read the bridge book. She took two lessons at the Y. Then she fell out the door of the laundromat. She came staggering in, her French twist askew and her stockings torn. "There was a step there," she said. "I didn't see it." At first, she limped around the house like it didn't matter, but pretty soon her ankle started swelling. "You should go to the doctor," I said. "They wouldn't do any good," she said. I heard her on the phone talking to Miss Bonnie. "Cost twenty dollars," she was saying. She got an Ace bandage from the drugstore and put it on her ankle, but it didn't get any better. Miss Bonnie, who also worked downtown, drove her to and from the office. She couldn't go play bridge, and, at any rate, Mary Lyles wasn't playing any more. "Mary's in the hospital," she said. "She has something the matter with her lungs." We were in the kitchen when she said this, and Mama was sitting in a chair because her ankle, which had red streaks coming up from it, hurt too much to stand.

The next day she got in a car with Miss Bonnie. "We're going to the hospital," she said, "to see Mary, and then I'm going to get something for my leg."

I thought she meant she was going to see a doctor, but when she came back, she was carrying a sack and a bottle of vinegar. The sack turned out to be full of red dirt. "Mrs. Wilton told me about this," she said excitedly, pouring the vinegar into the dirt. "You mix red clay with vinegar and it acts like a poultice." Mrs. Wilton, Miss Bonnie's mother, had also told them to get the red clay from where they were building the interstate. "How was Mary Lyles?" I asked. Mama laughed. "She says from her room she can see the graveyard." The red clay actually worked; the red streaks disappeared. By the time Mary Lyles died, Mama was able to drive herself to the funeral. She never learned to play bridge.

The second bad thing that happened in 1963 was that Miss Rolla didn't die. Tommy had tried his best, and I had suggested that he try again using an Irish potato, but he appeared to have given up.

Without Tommy's scientific insights, class became, if possible, more boring. I wasn't able to liven things up, either. No matter how many interesting comments I made, I couldn't get anybody's attention, unless I had happened to break one of the rules. For show-and-tell one morning, I waved my hand and announced, "My mother hurt her ankle, and she went to where they're building the interstate and got red clay to put on it and it got well." Everybody just looked at me. That was the last time I said anything in class, except for telling Harry Falk to drop dead.

Once Mama's ankle got better, she signed up to take the bar exam. She was already a member of the Mississippi Bar, but she had never bothered getting her Alabama license. Since my father had died, she wasn't supposed to be practicing law. "After I pass the bar," she said, "we won't have to worry about money."

About the time Mama started studying for the bar, Libby quit. She had been telling Ray, Clay, and me all along that she was leaving as soon as her grandmother died, but apparently she hadn't told Mama, who was pretty surprised one morning when Libby arrived in a car instead of on the bus and came in long enough to say that her grandmother had died and she was leaving. Then she left, since her ride was waiting. Clay, who like the rest of us had known Libby all his life, started to cry. "Don't you dare cry," said Mama. I have no idea what they did with my chicken.

After Libby left, Granny watched us after school. During the summer, said Mama grimly, we would go to the Y. Since the Y had a trampoline, this could have been worse. Meanwhile, in order to save time, Mama bought a bunch of frozen Swanson's dinners and that's what we had to eat every night while she studied. Granny took a dim view of these meals: "old tinfoil mess." The plates they came in were sort of interesting, though, divided into sections so gravy wouldn't get all over your food.

Mama took the bar review course from Jones Law School downtown. She usually came in smelling like smoke. "Those men all smoke cigars," she said, fanning herself. When I heard her talking on the phone to Miss Bonnie, she sounded worried. "Tax," she kept saying.

The bar exam took three days. At the end of the first day, I looked out the kitchen window to see Mama just sitting in the car, in the driveway. When I opened the car door, she just kept sitting there. "I can't go back," she said.

Since Mama didn't pass the bar, she started working as a legal secretary for different law firms around town. Lobman, who had been the ringleader of my father's gambling friends, offered her a job as his confidential secretary, but she didn't take it. Right after this I over-heard her talking to Miss Bonnie on the phone. I couldn't be sure she was talking about this job, which had sounded glamorous to me, because all she said was "another think coming."

We spent the summer at the Y pool, and then I had to start sixth grade. I hadn't thought it could be any worse than fifth grade, and in fact it wasn't, though in a way sixth grade was just as bad. The teacher, Miss Tyler, was determined to teach us manners. The boys caught the worst of it, having to spend a whole morning pulling out chairs for the girls, the trick being not to yank the chair out from under us just as we sat down. The manners lessons might have worked better if she had started with something simple, like trying to get us to stop being so mean. There were several kids who were being picked on nonstop: Hiram Couch, because it turned out his middle name was Percival; Patrick McGehee for stuttering; me, for a variety of fairly vague reasons; and Becky Fry, because she had freckles and had lived in Hawaii. I think if Becky hadn't happened to have mentioned Ha-waii she might have been all right, although she would still have had freckles. Maureen Clements, meanest girl in school, was the leader of the anti-Becky forces. Every time she saw Becky Fry, she would yell "Hey, French Fry!!" which would have made more sense if Becky had lived in France. In a way, I owed Becky a favor; thanks to her, I was no longer the last to be chosen for kickball, though Harry Falk and his assistant Wally Gold were still on my case twenty-four hours a day for offenses including wearing glasses and over-salting my food. At this point, it was almost as if the school building itself was radioactive and making everybody who came in contact with it act like a jackass.

I realized how bad things had gotten one Saturday. I happened to be in a car with Becca Hollis and her mother when we spotted Becky Fry sneaking furtively along the sidewalk. In unison, Becca and I promptly yelled "Hey, French Fry!!!" Becky didn't even look surprised. Mrs. Hollis was very annoyed. "Rebecca!" she intoned. "I didn't raise you to make mean remarks to people and I'm sure," she added to me, not sounding very sure at all, "that your mother didn't either."

Right after this incident, there was a bright spot: I discovered a way to escape going to the school library. We had to go once a week for an hour, during which time we were under the jurisdiction of Miss Miranda Peale, who had squinty glasses and a frizzy perm. She also had the distinction of having been evicted from an apartment building my parents had once owned for, according to my mother, acting like she had a chip on her shoulder. I didn't like going to the library because it didn't have any good books and because Miss Peale watched me like a vulture the whole time, just waiting for me to do something so she could evict me.

So one day, instead of going to the library, I hid. It was really pretty easy. There was a piano sitting in the hall and I just got out of line and crouched behind it until everyone had passed, then wandered off in the opposite direction. Then I had to figure out what to do. I wound up going in the auditorium. There was nobody in there. It was cool. It was quiet. There was a clock. I could just stay there until time to go back to class.

I sat and pondered. Why on earth had I yelled that at Becky Fry? How would I feel if it was me? My reasoning didn't go any further, since about this time I was brought up short by the thought that, nine times out of ten, it was me.

The auditorium was a good place to think and relax, but unfortunately I got caught the third week because I neglected to allow for the possibility that the seventh graders might be in there rehearsing their part in the Veterans' Day assembly. There they were, all lined up on stage, wearing sheets with big crosses on them and reciting, in unison, "In Flanders Fields." I made an attempt to escape but was apprehended by their teacher, Mrs. Golan, who dragged me back to Miss Tyler's room. Everybody was surprised, since they hadn't noticed I was gone. Miss Tyler, glaring, sent me back to the library under Becca's custody. I thought maybe Becca would let me escape.

I tried talking to her. "I don't know what she's so upset about," I said. Becca stared straight ahead. Apparently she didn't want to be charged with being an accomplice. Becca deposited me at the door of the library, wheeled, and left. Instead of turning myself in to Miss Peale, I left, too.

I should have gone back to class. Instead, I walked through the door back of the auditorium stage. There was a table sitting there, and someone had pulled plywood sheets up to three sides of it. Another piece of plywood was leaning against the fourth side. I crawled under the table and pulled the plywood up to the edge. It was dark in there, and it smelled like chalk and dust, but it was peaceful, sort of like being under the bed. Eventually, I would have to come out, and I wasn't sure what my next move should be. I doubted I could talk to Mama. Not being able to face the bar exam was not really the same thing as not being able to face your entire life.

It had been a very bad year, but surely, I thought, the worst is over. There wasn't time for anything else bad to happen now; 1963 was practically finished. It was just a couple of weeks until Thanksgiving.

WORSE THAN

We were at Dickie Pate's house when he started talking about some guy in the movies called Private Prescott who was, he said, worse than Sergeant York. He didn't know much else about this guy except that he lived in Canada. I wondered how a private got to be worse than a sergeant and decided that whatever he did had been so bad that they'd demoted him. Later I saw something in the paper about a movie called *Sergeant Preston of the Yukon* and thought that it was possible Dickie had gotten it wrong.

Brenda Dobbs was a more dependable source of information about things that were worse than other things. The hydrogen bomb, she announced, was one hundred times worse than the atom bomb. That was pretty much common knowledge but then she came out with something surprising. A wolverine, she said, was like a wolf only worse. This was an alarming thought, although it turned out that wolverines, like Private Prescott, lived in Canada. A wolverine was worse than a wolf, said Brenda, because wolverines could climb trees, leaving you no means of escape. I thought that Canada must be a complete hellhole.

We were walking home from school one winter day when Brenda offered some information that was even more alarming than the news on wolverines. I had been plodding along, head down, reliving a scene of humiliation that had occurred during current events that day when she caught up to me. "*Outer Limits*," she said breathlessly, "is worse than *Twilight Zone*."

The Twilight Zone was bad enough. I had particularly disliked the episode where the guy looks out the plane window and there is a gremlin on the wing, especially since Dickie Pate's father, who was in the air force, said there were such things as gremlins, and pilots were always having trouble with them.

As far as *The Outer Limits* went, I was willing to take Brenda's word for it, but my brothers were friends with Brenda's brother Bobby, and they wanted to watch *The Outer Limits* with him, so I went, too.

My mother was not enthusiastic about us going to the Dobbs house because she said the Dobbses were trash. The main evidence of this was Mr. Dobbs, who had a tattoo of an anchor and was usually drunk. The fact that they were from Georgia pretty much clinched it.

There wasn't anything particularly trashy going on when we got there, but it wasn't even seven o'clock yet. I felt a little apprehensive, since the Dobbses' house had one scary feature which, as far as I could tell, had nothing to do with being trashy: an old lady who would pop out from a pitch-black room, fix you with a wild glare, then suddenly retreat. The crone was Mr. Dobbs's mother who, said Brenda, had been in Bryce Hospital. I wondered if she had escaped.

On this particular evening, the old lady appeared, glared, and vanished just as I got in the door, leaving us to get on with our television viewing.

It had been decided that since *The Outer Limits* was so scary as to be life-threatening, we should all get under a quilt, and one of us would look out regularly to give an update on the episode. I shot a last despairing look at the television, which was located right under the Dobbses' picture window, and submerged myself under the quilt. I could hear the narration. "You do not know these men," intoned an official voice that sounded worse than Rod Serling's. The sound was muffled, though, so when Brenda, whose turn it was to look, said "Gah!" and suddenly reappeared under the quilt, we were all surprised.

"It's these guys," she said. "They've got aliens and they stick them on people's backs."

"How they do that?" asked Bobby, sounding exasperated.

"Because they look like crabs," said Brenda.

"Yeah, sure," Bobby went topside. In no time flat, he was back. "These aliens look like crabs and then they get in your brain," he said excitedly, "and then you go crazy."

"Go back out!" said Ray, feeling we were missing something.

"No way. You go," said Bobby.

Ray, who didn't seem happy about it, surfaced. There was an interlude, during which I noticed how the dim light under the quilt made people's faces look scary. Then Ray reappeared. "A woman ran over the guy!" he said. "She was one of the crabs! He broke his leg! Now he's crawling and trying to get away!"

"Go back out!" we yelled.

Ray refused point blank. "It's Clay's turn," he stated. Clay wasn't having any. "It's Kathie's turn."

"Yeah, go on." Reluctantly, I stuck my head out. The beleaguered guy, who I guessed was the hero, was crawling down a road. Unfortunately, an alien crab was also crawling down the road, straight for him. I averted my eyes. The Dobbses had a floodlight in front of their house; the picture window was lit up, almost like a television screen. I stared at it. This was a mistake.

Against my will, I started reliving what had happened to me earlier that day in current events. I could see it in the picture window, plain as day. There I was, giving my dynamite report on Fidel Castro, the payoff for two weeks of research in the newspapers section of the Montgomery Public Library. I rattled my notebook paper, all five pages, with a flourish. "Fidel Castro," I read happily, "enjoys the distinction of having established a successful Communist government under the nose of the United States, less than ninety miles from the peaceful shores of Key West, Florida." I galloped enthusiastically along, covering Cuban politics, history, and geography to my final thought, finishing with a chilling "remains to be seen!" It was at that point that I began feeling uneasy. Miss Tyler was glaring at me. In fact, she looked quite a bit like the crab woman on television who was now aiming her car once more at the hero. "What did she do, class?" hissed Miss Tyler. There was a deathly silence. Nobody wanted to guess what I had done, least of all me. "She . . . read . . . it," continued Miss Tyler. "She . . . Didn't . . . Memorize . . . It."

Oh. Right. So I sat back down.

Now, brooding, I wondered if you could classify everything into things that were worse than other things. Private Prescott was worse than Sergeant York. Wolverines were worse than wolves. *The Outer Limits* was worse than *The Twilight Zone*.

School was worse than *The Outer Limits*.

On the screen, there was a burst of gunfire. I yawned.

Abruptly, Brenda grabbed my arm and dragged me back under. "What all was happening?" she demanded. Under the quilt, her face was purple. She was sort of pop-eyed. She looked almost like a crab.

I shrugged. "It's okay. It had a happy ending. Some guys with guns shot the crab woman just in time."

I could hear, dimly, the announcer repeating mournfully, "You do not know these men," as the closing theme music started.

"It was really scary, though," said Brenda forcefully. "Worse than *Twilight Zone*, right?"

I nodded. "Worse than anything," I said. "Pretty much."

CONTENTED

We got Abicat courtesy of an act of meanness by a kid named Winton Flowers. One day in sixth grade Winton mentioned that one of his cats had had kittens. I told my mother about it and she said I could ask for one. So I did, and Winton said he was keeping them all. Mama thought that was the meanest thing she had ever heard. Really, it wasn't even in the top twenty-five as far as I was concerned. Winton probably intended refusing me a kitten as a mean gesture, but he was telling the truth; every time we drove past his house there were two or three dozen cats sitting out front.

We gave up on trying to get a free kitten. Instead we went to a pet store near Oak Park and inspected a whole cage full of kittens, reasonably priced at one dollar each. I wanted an orange one, because of a picture book I had entitled *The Contented Little Pussy Cat,* about an orange cat named Abner. However, the only orange kitten turned out to be a female and was vetoed by my mother, so we wound up with a fairly fluffy black and white model. We named him Abner anyway and took him home, where we put him in a peach basket to sleep on the back porch. He meowed until I went out there and lay down next to him.

I thought of Abicat as my first real pet. I'd had a goldfish named Jack and two guppies named Fred and Ethel, but they weren't big on interaction. There was a short-lived experiment with a gray kitten before I was old enough to go to school. This kitten didn't even get a name before one or both of my brothers slung him/her around by the tail; he/she went off to live with Libby's grandmother, in what I'm sure the kitten saw as a miraculous rescue.

By the time Abner got there, we were all old enough to behave. The first thing we did was to modify his name. Abner didn't suit him; Abicat did. He may have been taken away from his mother too young; at any rate, he was fixated on my mother, crying until she picked him up. He would also just sit and gaze up at her, drooling. His tastes were eclectic; he liked turnip greens and chocolate cake. My mother would bake especially for him some sort of very cheap fish that smelled terrible, wrapping the fish in aluminum foil that we had to bury behind the garage because it smelled too bad to go in the garbage can.

The summer after I finished sixth grade, Abi was an accidental participant in what could have been a momentous event. My mother had been just forty-one when my father died, and she was beautiful, with black wavy hair and green eyes—and, as Lee once noted, a shape like a Coca-Cola bottle. Once my father died, all the married couples she knew quit inviting her to parties, though the husbands would sometimes drop in on her at work. I found this out by eavesdropping. Whenever Mama pulled the phone in the kitchen and shut the door, she was usually talking to Miss Bonnie about something interesting. By listening at the door, I could pick up a stray phrase, like "perfectly obvious" or "got his nerve." In addition to the husbands, my mother had an admirer from her youth who had contacted her after he got a divorce. "Poor Henry," said Mama to Miss Bonnie. I had found out that Henry lived in Mississippi when my mother, during a fight with Granny, stormed out to the backyard where I was putting fertilizer on strawberries and said, "How would you like to move to Mississippi?"

I mumbled something about having to leave all my Montgomery friends, which was nonsense; really I was thinking it was an unfair question. Why couldn't she ask whether I'd like to move to Gulf Shores?

Then one summer day, Henry actually showed up. He was a preacher, which I didn't find out until he was on the way to the house. I thought that might be all right; since he was a preacher, he probably wasn't as bad-tempered as my father. In fact, he might be completely nonviolent. He turned out to be a tall gangly man who seemed to be roughly a hundred years old, or at least in his late forties. He sat in the living room talking to Mama; Ray and Clay had fled and were sequestered in their room with Abi, who was taking a catnap. "All right," I said, "if this guy is going to hang around here, he needs to meet Abicat." Henry had presumably already met Granny, who was in the backyard, muttering. I picked up Abi, who mewed confusedly, and we hauled him into the living room. By this time he weighed somewhere around ten pounds and was a long cat; it took two of us to carry him. "Here's our cat, Abi," I said happily. Henry was not impressed. "What you want to go dragging that ol' cat in here for?" he asked, then laughed raucously, as if he'd said something witty. I glanced at Mama. Her eyes had narrowed. That was the last we heard of poor Henry, or of Mississippi.

The following October, when Abi turned one year old, we decided to give him a birthday party. We invited all sorts of kids. A few of them came, including Ellis and Till Chalmers. Since the Chalmerses lived in a big mock-Tudor house full of antiques and Mrs. Chalmers was famous for going around saying that her grandmother had danced with Jefferson Davis, I suppose it shouldn't have come as a surprise that Ellis and Till had brought Abicat a nice present, but even so I was floored when, after a number of catnip mice and balls of yarn had been unwrapped, they came up with a silver serving spoon and tray designed to be used with canned cranberry sauce. This was not what you ordinarily gave a cat, even a Persian: I was extremely impressed. Not until later did it occur to me that Mrs. Chalmers's cranberry server might have left her silver chest without permission. Meanwhile, Thanksgiving was just around the corner.

"Thanks!" I said, on behalf of Abicat. "This'll come in handy."

COUNTRY CLUB

At a certain point, I started noticing that I wasn't exactly speaking the same language as some of the other kids. For example, in third grade Becca Hollis invited me to her house for dinner. I was confused. "Do you mean dinner in the middle of the day, or do you mean supper?" She meant supper.

Even the way we talked was different. I was at Jenny Craven's house waiting for my mother to come get me from scouts when Melissa Jones's mother started talking with Mrs. Craven about a costume pageant the Junior League had held at the country club. "The curtain goes up and there"—Mrs. Jones swung her arm dramatically, narrowly missing me—"was Barbara Ellerbach sittin' on a bar stool, smokin' a cigarette and drinkin' a beer!" Mrs. Craven laughed appreciatively, but I was less interested in Mrs. Ellerbach's theatrical debut than in the fact that Mrs. Jones had pronounced the last three words as "darankin' uh beeyah!" There was no doubt about it; people at our house spoke with a sort of twang, while almost everybody else we knew talked like they were drunk. This was a little worrisome, since the way we talked was sort of like the way the Dobbs family talked, and they were trash.

Our house was different too. We had only one bathroom, and one window-unit air-conditioner, located in our parents' bedroom. We had a floor furnace instead of central heat. We had some things other people had, but not everything. We had a color television; we didn't have a colander.

My grandmother was the only person I knew who dipped snuff.

Our social fate was really sealed, though, by the fact that we didn't belong to the country club. We weren't the only ones. Sarah Stein said that the country club wouldn't let Jews join, so for revenge all the Jews in Montgomery had gotten together and started their own club, after which they had hired the country club's head cook and all the waiters. I thought this was pretty good.

The main problem with not belonging to the country club was not having a place to go swimming, but we had fixed that by joining the Y. It had a nice pool, almost as good as the one at the country club, said Becca, who used to go swimming with me once a week in the summer.

Although I hadn't been inside the country club, I had been to the parking lot. Becca's mother had driven me, Becca, and Becca's little brother to see the Fourth of July fireworks display from the parking lot back of the golf course. Mrs. Hollis was in a fairly bad mood; she poured something from a Boy Scout canteen into a paper cup and sat there drinking and muttering. The fireworks were pretty good, although you could see them nearly as well by sitting on the curb in front of our house. At one point, Becca's brother got out of the car and banged the car door into the car next to us.

"Hey!" yelled the guy in the car. "You kids watch it! You hit my door."

Mrs. Hollis roared into life. "Take your damn car and go home if you don't like it!"

I automatically dropped to the floor, covering my head, but there was no follow-up. The guy piped down. Maybe he recognized her.

One spring day in sixth grade, Becca Hollis walked up to a bunch of us at recess. "I'm having a birthday party at the country club," she said, "and you're all invited. You can order anything you want," she added enthusiastically. "You can even order steak." I laughed. "Right," I said, my usual rejoinder whenever anybody said anything stupid. I knew all about steak. First you had to beat it with a rolling pin to make it tender, then you dunked it in flour and fried it in grease from the can on the back of the stove. And you still had to chew for five or ten minutes before you could swallow it. However, a place like the country club was bound to have something fit to eat; maybe meatloaf.

My mother was enthusiastic about Becca's invitation, but seemed worried I would get out of line, because she kept cautioning me to sit up straight and not talk with my mouth full. She needn't have worried.

Miss Tyler was giving the entire class a crash course in manners, using the same book she had studied in 1910. She had also made us learn to waltz, though I didn't see what good that would do me at lunch.

I was looking forward to Becca's party, partly because I envisioned myself swimming in the country club's Olympic-sized pool. On the day of the party, I took the precaution of wearing my swimming suit under my blue taffeta dress, just in case.

The country club was a big low building surrounded by an enormous golf course. We climbed out of Becca's mother's car, filed into a long room lined with windows, and sat at an incredibly big table set with white china and cloth napkins, with little vases of flowers at each place. There was a huge chandelier over the table. Sarah Stein looked around and shrugged.

I glanced through the longest menu I'd ever seen, finally ordering something made with lobster and sherry. It turned out to be nothing to write home about—odd-tasting and rubbery, though not as chewy as steak. Sarah had ordered the same thing. "This new cook of theirs," she said happily, "isn't much."

After lunch, Becca showed us the locker rooms, but the pool was empty.

The man in charge said it wouldn't open until next week.

Even empty, I could tell the country club pool was a lot better than the one at the Y. It was huge. You could put a battleship in there. Also their locker room had carpet and a TV.

Though I thought Becca had given me a funny look about the steak, we stayed friends until we got to junior high school the following year. We were still in the same public school, but the students whose parents belonged to the country club were now going to parties and dances and something called Junior Assembly, which was a sort of dress rehearsal for being a debutante. When Becca had her next birthday party, I wasn't invited. In fact, I didn't realize she'd had a party until I overheard some people talking about it.

A few days later, I was looking through a drawer and found my snapshot album from first grade. There was Becca, looking solemn. I read what I had written. My Best Friend—Becca Hollis. My Favorite Actress—Martha Raye. My Favorite Sport—swimming.

I suddenly realized that I hadn't been swimming all year.

Ramon and Virginia Ferguson Farnell, 1950.
All photographs are from the author's collection.

Mama and Granny: no love lost

Aunt Katherine and Kathie

Clay and Ray in the barbecue pit

Ray and Lee

First day of school: note the expression

Mona at a truck stop

Granny, Libby, a watermelon, Daddy

Ray, Kathie, Clay, and Abicat at the piano

Last day of school, Kathie at bottom right: note the expression

OUTDOORS

Ray and Clay joined the Boy Scouts, but it didn't work. The troop met at Holy Comforter Episcopal Church, the second-most snobbish Episcopal church in town, so you would think the scouts would be pretty staid. Instead, on their first campout at the lake they pitched their tents at a spot which happened to be within easy walking distance of Junior Hood's uncle.

I am not sure why Junior Hood joined scouts, unless he was considered too young for the Ku Klux Klan. At any rate, according to Ray, Junior Hood's uncle was eighteen years old and lived in a trailer on the side of a gravel pit. While the scoutmaster was at an adjoining campsite investigating rumors of a snake, the entire troop with the exception of the senior patrol leader followed Junior through the woods. Junior's uncle had welcomed his nephew and the other scouts effusively, calling off his dogs and producing a gallon jug which had once contained Clorox. "Long as I got a acre, you got a acre," he informed Junior generously.

Mama, when the incident was reported, was not impressed. "That was that jug talking," she said.

Junior Hood was booted from the scouts even though Ray and Clay thought it had been the best campout ever. After that, all the scouts did was tie knots, and Ray and Clay soon lost interest.

The three of us were pretty well used to being left up to our own devices when it came to exploring the outdoors. Montgomery was not an easy place to commune with nature. For one thing, the city park had been closed due to integration for as long as any of us could remember. The closest thing we had to a park was Greenwood Cemetery, where we went to pick blackberries. Greenwood was fairly peaceful, but it wasn't perfect. For one thing, some of the urns were home to hornets. For another, the cemetery was the headquarters of a roving gang of swans, all of whom were apt to come honking after you if you wandered onto their turf.

I suppose I could have continued camping with the Girl Scouts, but I had pretty much given up on scouts once junior high started. Annette and Patty still belonged, wearing uniforms that looked like

97

something a stewardess would have worn about 1954. Once I went on a campout to Panama City with their troop, but it was not an unqualified success. For one thing, the scout leader, Mrs. Landers, had to tell the guy at the entrance to St. Andrews State Park that we were a family reunion in order to get to camp there, and I don't think he believed her. For another thing, Annette had leftover fried chicken in the tent in case she got hungry in the middle of the night, and the food attracted raccoons. Once you added in the fact that all the toilets had backed up, I didn't see any real reason to continue camping out.

None of us seemed cut out for organized outdoor activities. We had once formed the Golden Leaf Club, which was dedicated to climbing other people's magnolia trees, and it had been moderately successful until people noticed us and started threatening to call the police.

Then there was the Firebugs. The Firebugs was a club, or gang, of people interested in setting fire to things. Ellis Chalmers, the founder, had elected himself president. I was never sure why Ray and Ellis were best friends, since they didn't have a whole lot in common. Ellis lived in a big house full of portraits of constipated-looking people, and Mrs. Chalmers, who looked like a less-friendly version of Queen Victoria, spent most of her time playing bridge. I could understand Ellis's younger brother Till being friends with Clay, since neither one of them talked. Over the years, it developed that the main thing Ray and Ellis had in common was the hobby of setting things on fire. In this one area, my family had something the Chalmerses lacked: a floor furnace which caught fire whenever Ray threw crayons down it. All Ellis had was central heating, and he may have organized the Firebugs as a way to make up for it. So far, my main contribution to the club had consisted of designing the official sign, which featured a roach striking a match. This was not as good as the official sign of The Fiends, a rival club whose sign depicted the devil smoking a cigarette and drinking a beer, but it was the best I could do considering the subject matter. One of the many problems with the Firebugs as an organization was the difficulty members had in finding a secluded spot to set things on fire.

Fortunately, there was one easily accessible spot of wilderness in Montgomery: The Ditch, conveniently located behind Ellis Chalmers's house. The Ditch had been a creek once. Even though it was surrounded by houses, it was still usually full of water. To get to The Ditch, you walked through some people's yards, which was relatively easy as long as no one spotted you. We usually didn't have to worry about Mr. and Mrs. Chalmers, but sometimes we had to hide to avoid Ellis's grandmother, who was known as Nanny. Thanks to Mrs. Chalmers, everyone in Montgomery now knew that Nanny's mother had once danced with Jefferson Davis. Despite this achievement, Mr. Chalmers didn't like Nanny, who had moved from her crumbling mansion downtown to an apartment carved out of the Chalmerses' house. Every time Mr. Chalmers got drunk, he would tell everyone his opinion of Nanny, which was, "We should have just let her die, back in 1947." I never did figure out what had happened back then.

The best way to avoid Nanny was to crawl through some bushes until you could climb over the Chalmerses' back fence, after which you had a relatively clear path to The Ditch, provided you stayed out of the briers.

Once you reached The Ditch, you might as well have been on the set of a Tarzan movie. Huge trees lined the banks, and most of them had big vines hanging down into the water. The place was ideal, in fact, for playing Tarzan. I did not think of myself as too old to play Tarzan. After all, Tarzan was grown. It wasn't like I was trying to play Mighty Mouse. However, if I ever felt I was too old to play Tarzan, I planned to switch to Marlin Perkins Wrestles the Giant Anaconda, which I had recently seen on *Wild Kingdom*. The Ditch was usually a reliable source of entertainment. In fact, the main thing that got in the way of playing Tarzan was Ellis's habit of suddenly deciding to do something related to the Firebugs.

One fall afternoon some of us were sitting around at The Ditch when Ellis announced he had found something good to set on fire. I felt a little uneasy. Only the week before, Ray and Clay had been sitting on Larry Nix's porch when a fire-related incident occurred. Frank, Larry's brother, had been in the backyard setting fire to little plastic army men when his can of lighter fluid backfired. As Ray reported later, "Frank came running around the side of the house on fire, not saying anything."

As soon as Frank recovered the power of speech, he had yelled, "Put me out! Put me out!" Ray, Clay, and Larry had responded to this request by falling off the porch laughing. Eventually, Frank had put himself out, but I still felt that setting fire to something, however good, might be a bad idea.

I had to admit, though, that Ellis had found something interesting, a perfectly intact umbrella he had spotted under a bush. "Watch this," said Ellis. He opened the umbrella, lit it, and twirled it around his head. "Singin' in the rain," sang Ellis. He would undoubtedly have gone into a dance if the umbrella, which was now ablaze, had not collapsed on him.

As Ellis and the remains of his umbrella sloshed around in The Ditch, I shook my head. You wouldn't catch Tarzan doing something like this.

CLAY RUNS AWAY

"Clay's just not a member of the family," Mama would say mournfully. This was true, but the odd thing was he actually looked like her side of the family, if you went back far enough. He looked like an Indian. This was probably part of the problem; he didn't resemble Ray or me.

Mama wasn't referring to Clay's looks, however, but to his habit of spending every waking minute at Bobby Dobbs's house. I didn't see the attraction. Not only was the Dobbs family universally reputed to be trash, Mr. Dobbs was at least as big a drunk as Mr. Chalmers, with the added liability of not belonging to the country club. Then there was Mr. Dobbs's mother, the crazy old bat who lurked in the back of the house. It was kind of like *The Addams Family* without the entertainment value.

It was true that Clay was on a different wavelength from the rest of us. Once Mama was attempting to explain why doctors sterilized instruments, and Clay asked if you would get deader if they cut you with an unsterilized knife. Another time, the radio was playing a song with the lyric "girls grow up faster than boys do," and Clay happily began singing along: "Girls don't go for assassinated boyfriends."

It may have been due to our reaction when he came out with one of these utterances that Clay didn't talk a lot, though after my father died he sort of perked up. He was an early fan of the Beatles (or Bettles, as he spelled it in a birthday card to Bobby). By the time I was in seventh grade and he was in fourth, he had let his hair grow into a luxuriant mop. Mama, in response to someone's remark about how my father would react to the hair, just shrugged, "Well, it's Clay's hair, isn't it?"

Despite her hands-off attitude toward the hair, Mama brooded about Clay's aversion to hanging around the rest of us and about his grades. "Maybe," she told Miss Bonnie, "I should just see if I could afford to send him to Williams."

This was serious. Williams School was a sort of combination reform school and military academy located in an old house in downtown Montgomery. Students there had to wear uniforms; the place would undoubtedly take a dim view of Clay's hair.

Clay may have sensed that something was up, because one day in early spring he and Bobby Dobbs ran away. It had started out to be such a good day, too. The weather was nice and I had had no trouble at all convincing Mama that I was too sick to go to school. I was in the backyard looking at some anemic tulips that came up reliably every year near the oleander when the door flew open and Mama emerged, looking harried. "Clay's left school," she said, "with Bobby. They didn't come here, did they?"

I shook my head. This was worrisome. I could understand leaving school but didn't see why anyone would go anyplace other than home to watch television. "Maybe they're at Bobby's," said Mama.

They weren't at Bobby's. Assisted by Bobby's mother, a haggard woman named Connie May who wore her jet-black hair in a ponytail, we searched the entire house, including Mr. Dobbs's ham-radio room, the shed where they kept the pet raccoon, and crazy Old Lady Dobbs's cave. Brenda, Bobby's older sister, sat on the edge of the rickety porch steps, chewing gum worriedly. There was some talk of calling Mr. Dobbs at the machine shop, but Connie May vetoed it. "No use worryin' him," she said, smiling nervously. Meanwhile, I was observing Old Lady Dobbs, who was muttering in the background. Was there any chance that she had been sent to Bryce Hospital for being a serial killer?

When we got back to the house, Ray was there, having been sent home to join the festivities. Mama cross-examined him, but he protested that he didn't know anything about Clay running away and didn't understand why Clay hadn't invited him to come along. Granny, meanwhile, was suggesting that we have the sheriff drag the river.

I went into the room Clay shared with Ray and sat disconsolately on the bed, accompanied by Abicat, who didn't seem worried since he went right to sleep. What if Clay had been killed by a serial killer? Looking around the room, I thought that he wouldn't leave much of a legacy. Most of the pile of stuff on the floor was Ray's, including a sign I had gotten him in Panama City: "Fight poverty. Throw rocks at a beggar." The only identifiable things of Clay's were a Beatles album and a little trophy he had gotten for jumping off the high dive at the Y. This epic jump had been just like Clay. While I hung back at the edge of the pool, worried that my father would decide to throw me in, Clay, five years old, marched up the ladder to the high dive and threw himself in, impressing the lifeguard so much that he had let Clay blow his whistle. Leaving school was just like him, too. I got out of school as often as possible by either being sick or by saying I was. Clay just left. It was possible, I thought, that the only people on earth who really understood Clay, not counting the Beatles, were the Dobbses and the people at the Y.

There was an idea. Maybe Clay had gone to the Y, though the outdoor pool wouldn't be open until May. I was about to suggest this to Mama, when she appeared in the doorway. "The sheriff found them," she said. Clay and Bobby had been walking along the railroad tracks headed, said the sheriff, for the cemetery.

This was the last straw as far as Mama was concerned. Not only was Clay not acting like a member of the family; now he was being morbid, too. Mama immediately pulled the phone into the kitchen and called Miss Bonnie. Listening through the door, I heard "straight to Williams School." Clay himself said very little. I wasn't sure what happened to Bobby but figured it was probably something violent, unless Connie May had somehow managed to keep Mr. Dobbs from noticing that Bobby had been gone.

A couple of days later, we went to the cemetery to put Easter lilies on my father's grave. He was buried between my Uncle Andy and Mary Sue Shackelford, no relation. Mary Sue was the mother of Cammie, my father's first wife, and had been peacefully reposing in a grave in Troy, Alabama, when Cammie had her dug up and reburied in our plot out of what Mama referred to as spite. When Cammie and my father divorced, Cammie left her mother where she was, so that we would have to pay for maintenance. Clay wandered off to sit on some other family's headstone, from which he gloomily surveyed the cemetery. Standing atop Mary Sue, I followed Clay's gaze. The cemetery was beautiful. There were huge camellia and azalea bushes in bloom by some of the graves. Trees in the background were full of purple wisteria. Just past the trees, there was a lake surrounded by white-flowering bridal-wreath bushes. This lake had a flock of angry swans and a rather frightening sculpture of Jesus popping out of his tomb, but I had to admit the whole effect was one of serenity and springtime beauty. In fact, the cemetery was the closest thing to a park that Montgomery currently had.

Looking at Clay, I thought I understood what had happened. When Clay and Bobby left school, neither one of them had much incentive to go home. Maybe Clay had just been looking for a little peace and quiet, and Bobby had tagged along because they were friends. Now Clay was getting sent to Williams School, and his hair was in jeopardy. I doubted that he could have seen this coming, but I didn't know, and Clay wasn't saying.

CUCKOO CLOCK

Lee had a cuckoo clock, though by the time I was born it had quit working. She had gotten the clock from a guy named Herbert, who was something of a legend. When Herbert, at the age of twelve, lost both parents, his one consolation was that he still had a roof over his head. Then he found out from an informant that evil relatives were plotting to take away his house. The same informant had advice for Herbert: get a white lawyer. Herbert had then presented himself at my parents' law office, announcing that although he was twelve years old and had no money, he could do yard work in exchange for legal services. My father was sympathetic; at the age of twelve, he had joined the U.S. Navy and gone off to fight in World War I, although he had been unmasked and ejected before the ship left Mobile. Herbert, his house saved, had done yard work for my family until he got old enough to enlist and had sent Lee the cuckoo clock from Germany. All this had happened years ago, but the cuckoo clock was still a major topic of conversation in Lee's neighborhood.

Lee lived near Catoma Creek, up a dirt lane behind the house of an old couple we called Uncle Milt and Aunt Katie; they were distinguished by having the only phone in the area. If you needed to talk to Lee, you called Uncle Milt and Aunt Katie, and at some point Lee would call you back. Lee called us in the spring of 1961, when Catoma Creek flooded. By the time we got there with a boat, she was marooned atop her dining room table. We had a home movie of Lee's pig being rescued; he had taken a dim view of riding in the boat. I had been worried about the cuckoo clock, but it was fairly high up on the wall. Lee's husband, Robert, was in no danger since he was downtown in jail.

After the flood, Lee's house went more or less back to normal. I visited her every once in a while, since she didn't live on a bus line, and my parents picked her up whenever she and Robert were coming to work in the yard or help with a barbecue, or whenever Lee went fishing with us. Lee's little house wasn't painted, but it had a porch. Inside, the rooms were in a straight line: living room, dining room— where the cuckoo clock was—bedroom, kitchen. Out back was the outhouse, a chinaberry tree, flowers, and the place where the pig lived. This pig looked gloomy, as if he had never really gotten over being in a boat. I used to talk to Lee about getting the cuckoo clock fixed, but neither of us knew anybody who fixed cuckoo clocks. In fact, neither of us knew anybody else who even had a cuckoo clock.

Lee got sick the year after my father died. I heard that she had gone to St. Jude hospital for a tumor. This didn't worry me, since I had misunderstood and thought Mama had said "tuna." Lee got better and we saw her for a while, but then the tumor came back. By this time Mary Lyles had died, and I had figured out that what Lee had was stomach cancer.

That spring, I was in seventh grade, though still in Cloverdale School, and things were changing. We had abandoned Morningview Baptist for First Methodist, right down the street, and that was an improvement, but a lot of changes were not for the better. One day, I listed everybody I knew who had died: Uncle Andy, Uncle Henry, Aunt Katherine, my father, Uncle Jule, Mary Lyles. Libby hadn't died, but she wasn't around anymore, although we did get a Christmas card. Things were changing around town, too. Nobody rode the bus.

The water fountain signs marked "White" and "Colored" were disappearing. These signs had confused us for years. We figured the water was coming from different tanks. One time Ellis Chalmers drank out of the colored fountain. He said it tasted the same, but we kept an eye on him for a couple of days, partly because Mrs. Chalmers would literally have killed him if he had embarrassed her by changing color.

At least they hadn't taken all the fountains out. When the library got desegregated, the city had taken all the tables and chairs out of the building. Then when Oak Park got desegregated, the city had closed the park, filled in the swimming pool, and shipped all the zoo animals to Birmingham. However, I thought grimly, if Cloverdale School ever got desegregated, there was no chance that they would just send us all home.

The school was full of rumors these days, and some of them distracted me from worrying about Lee. We first heard about the Selma march from the newspapers, but soon it became all anybody could talk about at recess. Thousands of people were said to be involved, all marching toward Montgomery, where they were planning a mass demonstration. Danny Thomas was reported to be among the marchers. I didn't see that it was his business. As the marchers crept closer to Montgomery, tensions rose, and finally the school itself got in the act.

My homeroom teacher was Mrs. Baisden, a redhead with a spectacular figure who was considered a goddess by the entire class. One morning, she walked to the front of the room and said, "I have an announcement from the principal." We shuddered inwardly. The principal's name was Mr. Slay, and it was an understatement. She read from a piece of paper. "All students are to remain in class. Do not leave school. Do not go to the demonstration."

We were completely confused. Why would a bunch of twelve-year-old kids want to go to a demonstration? At least the part about leaving school made perfect sense. At recess, the consensus was that this announcement was coming from the Board of Education and was aimed at the kids in the colored school who had, for all we knew, been looking forward to the demonstration for weeks.

There were two more items of news. Amy Sanders reported that her grandmother, who lived downtown, had had her azaleas ruined by a state trooper who rode a horse through her front yard; and someone else said the marchers were planning to camp at St. Jude.

This worried me, since Lee had been at St. Jude.

When I asked Mama about it, she said Lee was not at St. Jude any longer; she had been sent home. This sounded like an improvement, but it wasn't. "There wasn't anything else they could do for her," said Mama.

That night, we were watching a movie about the Alamo on television. Cannons were firing, people were falling off walls. It was pretty good. Granny wandered in, surveyed the screen, and muttered "It's them old marchers again."

Mama went to see Lee, taking her some Metrecal since, she said, Lee had trouble keeping food down. I asked if I could go. "You wouldn't want to see her," said Mama. "Lee's gotten so thin she doesn't look like herself." This was the strangest news yet. Lee was a big round woman; when I went to Belk's to get her a sweater for Christmas, I just asked for the biggest one they had. Now I thought that seeing Lee thin was probably better than not seeing her at all, but I didn't say anything because Mama seemed so preoccupied. "Downtown," she had said at supper, "is full of Yankees wearing sunglasses."

It was about this time that we started hearing drums. They would start up as soon as it got dark, always coming from the direction of Alabama State University, the black college that I only noticed when we drove past it to get to the curb market. The drums would go on for a couple of hours, then stop. Miss Bonnie happened to be visiting the second time we heard the drums. She paused on the doorstep. "What's that? It's coming from that school, isn't it?"

"I don't know," said Mama, looking a little worried. Miss Bonnie glared in the direction of the drums. "They're planning something. Do y'all have a gun?"

"No," said Mama, even though we did have that handgun Daddy had kept from his unsuccessful defense of a murder case.

Miss Bonnie shook her head. "You know," she continued confidentially, "they've instructed all white women to leave New York City." This was alarming. Where were all those white women supposed to go? New Jersey?

The following day I solved the mystery of the drums. I was flipping through the newspaper, which carried a large front-page photo captioned "Marchers" of some people standing in a road. The paper had a section called "Negro News," which was usually no more interesting that the white news. Today, however, I spotted a brief item in the "Social Whirl" column. "Congrats!" it began cheerfully, "To our Bama State Marching Band, which leaves next week for The Big Easy and the finals in the Spring Battle of the Bands Southeast Negro Division! Go get 'em, boys and girls!"

I took the paper to Mama. "They're practicing," I said; "that's all those drums are. That's just their band practicing."

I'm not sure she believed me. The next day was Saturday, and I was at the office with Mama when Mr. Russell came in. He was the Fuller Brush man, and he always made a beeline for Mama's office with a trunk load of free samples, grinning wildly all the while. He was just getting his case unfastened when the phone rang.

Mama answered it. "Aunt Katie?" she said, listened a minute, then said "I sure am sorry. Please tell Robert I'm sorry." She hung up the phone, caught my eye and shook her head. Mr. Russell was still sitting there beaming with his sample case open. "Well!" said Mama brightly. "Let's see what you've got here!"

A few days later, I asked Mama about Lee's funeral. She looked up from the paper; the headline, in extra-large letters, read "Marchers to Target Capitol."

"I don't expect we'll go," she said slowly. "I expect we'd feel sort of out of place somehow."

I went outside with Abicat and sat on the picnic table where Lee and I used to sit to crack pecans. I knew for a fact that Lee would have gone to my funeral, march or no march.

I wondered what would happen to her clock.

CAMP

To go to camp, you had to get a tetanus shot. That was enough to stop me. I thought volunteering to get a shot would be the stupidest move anybody could make, right up there with volunteering to go to summer school. It was kind of hard, though. Every year in spring we would have an assembly and Camp Grandview would put on a slide show and pass out brochures, all of which showed hundreds of kids having fun, and none of which showed kids getting shots. You found out about the shot in the fine print. Ray and Clay went to a day camp, Camp Belser, owned by the same rich family that owned Camp Grandview. They left each morning in a bus from Cloverdale School and arrived back in the afternoon, yelling their heads off with the rest of the campers. According to Ray, the most exciting thing that happened at Camp Belser, other than the discovery that the camp had been built over an Indian burial ground and was haunted, was the campwide frog race. The frogs were put in a circle and the first one to hop out won. Ellis Chalmers's frog had been in the lead until Ellis, jumping up and down in excitement, landed on him.

The closest I got to camp during this time was a one-night campout arranged, God knows why, by the Girl Scout troop. Just before I turned eleven, we had gone out to some land that Mrs. Craven's family owned at the lake. We had a list of things we were not supposed to bring, including comic books. This presented me with a dilemma: where was the best place to hide the comic book? I finally stuffed it into the bottom of my new Girl Scout sleeping bag. I didn't actually read the thing; I just liked knowing it was there. The highlights of the camping trip were Sarah Stein setting fire to the latrine by knocking over a lantern, me reaffirming that I didn't eat chili, and a rainstorm. Someone took a picture of me sitting on a huge fallen tree, wearing a raincoat and rain hat.

This experience, which should have cured me of wanting to go to camp, actually made me want to go to camp more. I figured actual camp had to be better. I didn't see any way around the tetanus shot, though, so by the time of my thirteenth birthday I was resigned to spending summer at the Y pool.

Then somebody at Sunday school handed me a brochure advertising Camp Blue Lake. We had switched to First Methodist Church from Morningview Baptist after my father died. I liked the Methodists better, because they were not always trying to make me get baptized and because the church building, only a couple of blocks from our house, was a lot bigger than Morningview and even had gargoyles, whereas Morningview still didn't even have a steeple.

The brochure looked almost as good as the one for Camp Grandview. The cover featured kids around a campfire. I read hurriedly through it, looking for the words "tetanus," "shot," or "inoculation," but I didn't see them. Apparently, you could go to the Methodist camp without having been shot for anything, even smallpox.

I had no idea where Camp Blue Lake was, but the brochure said the bus trip would take about two hours, so I brought a bag of potato chips. I didn't recognize any of the kids on the bus. Apparently everybody from First Methodist still went to Camp Grandview, probably figuring that otherwise they would have gotten a shot for nothing. After I got settled in my seat, I noticed that the girl in the seat in front of me looked sort of familiar. She had nondescript blonde hair, but her ears were unmistakable. They stuck out, making her look like Alfred E. Neuman. As the bus pulled out, she started singing "Woolly Bully." A lot of people joined in, sounding a little confused because nobody really knew what the words were. By this time I had figured out that the girl was Carol Willis and that she was in my gym class. Around the middle of the song, she apparently ran out of words she knew and launched into "House of the Rising Sun," which got mixed reviews. "This is a Christian camp," said a mean-looking redheaded girl. "So what," said Carol. I decided I would introduce myself as soon as she stopped singing.

When we got to the camp, there were two immediate surprises. One was that we weren't staying in tents. We were in cabins with screened windows and doors and a bathroom. The girls' cabins were on one side of the lake, the boys' on the other. The lake was the other surprise. It turned out to be sitting on top of an old graveyard, so the camp was haunted. I couldn't figure out who would put a lake on top of a graveyard, but finally decided it must have been Alabama Power.

That first night, I was able to grab a top bunk—I figured there was no use in having bunk beds if you didn't get a top one. Carol Willis had the top bunk right across from me. The mean redheaded girl, whose name was Janice, was right below me, which was depressing. It took me a while to get to sleep, since there were owls. The next thing I knew, somebody was hitting a gong. "Breakfast!" yelled Carol.

We filed into the cafeteria, which was also the assembly room.

I had never seen so much food in my life. At my house, if you opened the refrigerator, it wasn't exactly empty, but it would have stuff in it like buttermilk and rutabagas that nobody in their right mind would eat. At breakfast, we usually had eggs and grits, but between Mama telling me that I didn't eat enough to keep a bird alive and Granny reminding me that I was supposed to have died in infancy, I never had much appetite. At camp, people just ate. We sat at benches at a big long table loaded down with grits, bacon, sausage, biscuits, toast, scrambled eggs, pancakes, and orange juice. The first day, I had three helpings of everything. "For a skinny kid," said Carol, "you sure eat a lot."

"Thanks," I said.

At mail call, a couple of people got letters, and Janice got a post-card from, she said, her friends at church. I got three letters and two cards, all from my mother. One card, which had a cat on it, was signed "Abicat." "Wow," said Carol, "You get a lot of mail." "Yeah," I said, try-ing to look nonchalant. My mother had typed all the letters on her of-fice typewriter. "You even get typed letters," said Carol. Several people crowded in to look.

Luckily at this point a whistle blew. "Swimming!" somebody yelled. "Time for swimming!" I was great at swimming, but it turned out that we weren't just going to swim, we were going to play Horse. I would have to use strategy. "I'll be a rider!" I yelled. "I weigh less than anybody here!" This was true. Despite my breakfast, I probably weighed fifteen pounds less than Leigh Guy, who was the next thin-nest. Everybody wanted me on their team, which was quite a change from kickball. Carol wound up being captain of the Green Team, and she ordered me aboard a big guy named Tom. We should have been evenly matched with the Blue Team, which featured a little black-haired girl named Lois Prentiss and a guy named Fred Hoover who was shorter than Tom, but it turned out Tom was no good at all at being a horse. When I grabbed Lois's arm, Tom floundered and fell down too. I was kind of worried Carol would blame me, even though I had had a death grip on Lois, but she was determined to blame the whole thing on Tom. "That kid's a sissy," she muttered. "Hey kid! What's your name?" "Tom," said Tom. "Thomasina!" yelled Carol. This got a big laugh.

In the days that followed, we hung around the lake as much as possible, because it was hot in camp. When we went on a walk through the pines, it was a little cooler but the air was full of the smell of resin melting off the trees. The entire woods smelled like a can of turpentine. The only air-conditioned places were the infirmary and the camp store, which was usually full of counselors hiding from us while they drank Cokes. Carol made a few funny insulting remarks about the counselors for getting Cokes, which we only got every other day, and for being cool, but mostly she picked on Tom. Every time she saw him she yelled "Thomasina!" whether anybody else was around or not.

One night, there was a full moon. We were all sitting on the pier, trying to cool off. "Wow," I said. "Look at the moon." "Yeah," said Carol. "Looks just like one of Thomasina's falsies." It was funny, but the whole situation was starting to remind me of the way I usually treated Patty Harris. At any rate, the next day I sent Patty a postcard, and instead of writing "Having a good time. Glad you're not here," I wrote "Having a good time. I saw a snake." I looked both ways to see if anybody was watching before I put the postcard in the slot. I had written Mama every day and sent a postcard to Ray and Clay saying "This camp is haunted," but I was careful to make sure nobody, meaning Carol, saw me. I was already attracting enough attention by getting more mail than everybody else put together.

After I mailed the postcard, I stood in front of the bulletin board looking at the announcement that there was going to be a talent show Friday night. While I was looking, Carol came up.

"I'm going to be in the show," she said. "Listen to this." She had made up an original song to the tune of "Barges," a sentimental favorite with Girl Scouts. "Counselors," she warbled, "we would like to go with you. We would like to drink Co-Colas too." It was actually a pretty good song. "And guess what?" she said. "I come on at the end of the show—right after Thomasina!"

"Huh?" I said. "What's he gonna do?"

"I don't know. Something really sissy, I guess. Maybe he'll say a poem."

Friday night, the assembly room was crowded, partly because of a rumor that Carol was actually going to sing "Louie Louie." I was really glad I wasn't in the show, although when Fred Hoover got a lot of applause for playing the guitar, I had one fleeting moment when I regretted not telling jokes, since I knew some great ones.

I fanned myself with my program. Suddenly the lights went out, except for a spotlight trained on the stage. "And now," bellowed the voice of Mike Haverty, the head counselor, "Mr. Tom Morris and a very special dance!"

The spotlight swiveled around and came to rest on the corner of the stage. Music—jazz—started up from a hidden record player. A leg appeared, then the rest of Tom. He was covered in two enormous fans, which, it later developed, he had made from cardboard covered in crepe paper. He flapped the fans tempestuously at us. Everyone, including the counselors, fell out of their chairs laughing. Tom, deadpan, spun around, gave a farewell waggle of his fans, and floated off stage left.

Carol Willis singing "Counselors" might have been a hit, if only she had appeared ahead of Tom. As it was, people were still applauding, laughing, and talking when she got up on stage. The situation wasn't helped by Tom, who stuck his head out from behind the curtain and bowed about halfway through Carol's song.

The next morning I noticed I was having trouble getting my shorts to button, but I still ate two farewell helpings of pancakes.

Carol didn't say much going home. Once she turned around to glare at Tom, who was apparently telling jokes to a bunch of kids in the back of the bus, but other than that she just looked out the window.

At the bus station, I was met by Mama, Granny, Ray, and Clay. Mama said, "It seems like you've been gone a year." Ray and Clay wanted to know how I knew the camp was haunted if I hadn't seen anything, and even Granny was in a good mood. "You been eating a lot," she said approvingly.

When we got home, I went in the bathroom and got on the scales. Sure enough, I had gained five pounds.

"Now that you're home," said Mama enthusiastically, "what's the first thing you're going to do?"

I shrugged. "I think I'll go see Patty."

LIGHTS

Ray was the only one of us who liked Christmas. About the middle of July, he would start playing the Tennessee Ernie Ford Christmas album on the hi-fi. Clay was afraid of Santa Claus, and I could take him or leave him, especially since our fireplace had gas logs and no functional chimney, but Ray was such a fan that he paid five dollars for a Santa Claus candle that he lit every Christmas for years. When we got the Christmas tree, right after Thanksgiving, Ray always put himself in charge of a special deluxe ornament which had, inexplicably, a thistle painted on it. My contribution to trimming the tree was to stand back about six feet and hurl tinsel at it, in imitation of something I had seen on *The Honeymooners,* while Clay's approach to the occasion consisted of leaving and going to Bobby's.

After my father died, Christmas got a lot quieter around our house since we only had Mama and Granny mad at each other instead of my father, Mama, and Granny mad at each other. We also added a tradition: the lawyers Mama worked for would always give us a nice, if weird, Christmas present. One year it was a crystal decanter, the next year a silver chafing dish. They seemed to think we were running an upscale restaurant. The other major change to the celebration involved Abicat: he had his own Christmas stocking, though his main present was usually a can of sardines.

One Christmas tradition that lingered after my father died was driving around to look at the Christmas decorations. Loveman's Department Store always had an elaborate display featuring something like a robot Santa Claus in a space-age workshop. The VA hospital had a huge star lit up on the roof, and there was always a big Christmas tree downtown, next to the fountain on Court Street.

The decorations on people's houses, however, were the real attraction, partly because I couldn't imagine why they would go to that much trouble. The big houses in McGehee Estates, back of the country club, blazed with artificial candles in the windows, whole Christmas trees lit up on front lawns, and roof displays that sometimes involved an entire sleigh. As we drove around looking, I found myself brooding about our house's unfestive appearance. "How come we don't have decorations on our roof like that house?" I asked, indicating a mansion's rooftop tableau of Santa Claus waving to the Three Wise Men. "Because," gritted Mama, "that house belongs to a woman who doesn't have to work for a living." I really wasn't sure whether the lady of the house had slithered around on the roof in person to secure Santa to the gable, but I shut up about it. Anyway, I was really more interested in looking at the elaborate lights festooning doors, windows, and even chimneys.

The Christmas that I was in eighth grade, Ray was feeling particularly festive. One Saturday in early December, we had eaten lunch at the Francis Cafeteria next to Loveman's and were walking down to inspect their window display ("Christmas on Mars") when Ray spotted a sign in the window of Capitol Floral: "Big Christmas Grab Bag Sale! A Bagful of Assorted Decorations for Only One Dollar!"

Ray knew a bargain when he saw one. My mother agreed that a dollar was not a bad price for an entire bag of Christmas decorations. When we got home and dumped the paper bag out on the living room floor, we realized that the main thing these assorted decorations had in common was that they were all broken. Our grab bag included a cherub with a fatal head wound, a camel missing a hump, two reindeer with one antler each, and a gold poinsettia with only three petals. "What a gyp!" said Ray. He rallied, though, when we discovered some perfectly good Styrofoam blocks that had apparently been included by accident. These Styrofoam blocks were extremely useful in creating tabletop Christmas decorations. First we soaked them in water. Then we went into the neighbor's yard and got cedar, pine, and holly branches which we stuck in the Styrofoam. The decoration was topped with a red candle (some of these had been included in the bag, and a few weren't broken) and one of the busted cherubs or camels, artistically placed in the greenery so that you couldn't see what

114

was wrong with it. The whole festive creation was then placed on an aluminum-foil-covered plate so the wet Styrofoam wouldn't get on the table.

It looked jolly, I had to admit it.

At this point, Ray became unstoppable. He suggested we have eggnog. Mama was unclear about the exact recipe, but she figured that as long as you beat up some eggs and added milk and sugar, you had the basics covered. She frowned, though, when she sipped it from a Santa Claus mug Ray had gotten at the ten-cent store. "It needs something." We never kept liquor in the house, because of a family history that included both Mama's Uncle Jule, who set fire to his own house while under the influence of moonshine, and my father's late brother Andy, an affable man who had once gotten drunk and fallen off the pier at Atlantic City. However, Mama knew that eggnog had to include whiskey. "We'll go to Joe's Deli," she said firmly. This was unprecedented. Joe's Deli was an unprepossessing place located next to the ten-cent store. The only reason I ever went in there was to get a Polish sausage from a big jar by the cash register. Until now my mother had always stayed away from Joe's, referring to it as "that bar." Now she marched in, leaving us in the car, and in a few minutes marched out with a tiny bottle of bourbon which she kept in the kitchen cabinet and only brought out when we had eggnog. It made it taste a lot better.

Ray still wasn't satisfied. "We need lights," he said, right after we got the tree decorated. I pointed to the tree lights, all of which we had gotten to work. Our tree in fact looked one hundred percent better than Patty Harris's aluminum tree, which was lit only by a rotating lamp shining through colored cellophane, but Ray had something else in mind. "Outside lights," he said. He had a point. From the street our house did not radiate Yuletide cheer. We could put the porch light on, in which case passersby could see the wreath I had made in scouts from strips of dry-cleaning bag tied around a bent coat hanger, and if we had the drapes open it was possible to catch a glimpse of the tree, but that was about it. Most of the front yard, in fact, was taken up by a large popcorn tree which had sprouted on its own soon after my father, who disliked trees, died. I loved the tree, which was beautiful in fall, but any Christmas decorating scheme would have to take it into consideration.

"Let's put some lights on the popcorn tree," said Ray. This turned out to be easier said than done. You couldn't just stick an extra string of Christmas lights, assuming we had had one, on the tree, because they were, as Mama pointed out, inside lights and what we needed were outside lights. We harangued Mama until she agreed to go to the hardware store and get some outside lights. Then we had to get a three-dollar outside extension cord and a roll of electrician tape to secure the outside lights to the outside cord without electrocuting ourselves. When we got home with our bag of supplies, we faced another problem: where, exactly, were we going to plug in the lights?

"We'll plug them in on the porch," said Ray. This was not a bad idea. There was an electric outlet on the porch which had a reputation for delivering a nasty shock, but we managed to get the extension cord plugged in, then unreeled the cord all the way out the porch door, which we propped open with a brick, and across the flower bed to the popcorn tree. As long as nobody tried to mow the grass, we were in good shape. At this point, even Clay was getting enthusiastic. "Let me put the lights on," he begged. "Oh, all right," said Ray, probably surprised that Clay had said something. Clay struggled with the string of white lights, heaving them around in the tree. I doubted that the effect was going to look like much, but at least I'd be able to tell people at school that we had outside lights. Finally Clay gave up, and we plugged the lights into the extension cord, which snaked up the trunk of the tree, sealing the whole thing with electrician tape. The tree twinkled with random lights, but in daylight you couldn't really see them. "Okay," I said. "We'll unplug the tree on the porch and plug it back in when it's dark."

Eventually the sun went down, and we plugged the cord back in, then trooped out into the front yard, where we saw a tree twinkling with random lights. "No," said Clay. "You got to go down to the street to see it." We went down to the street, turned around, and were amazed. Seen from this angle, the lights formed the silhouette of a camel. One with two humps. It was plain as day.

Nobody knew quite how Clay had managed it, but for the time being, McGehee Estates had nothing on us.

CHOIR

Cloverdale's eighth-grade choir had won the regional competition, so we were headed to the state sing-off at the University of Alabama.

Mama was all excited. "You'll be able to see where I went to school," she beamed. We had, in fact, once gone to Tuscaloosa for a football game and had seen the focal point of Mama's college career: the steps leading up to the University Supply Store. Apparently, Mama had spent a lot of time sitting on these steps, surrounded by admirers. "It's a shame," Mama continued, "that you aren't going there in fall, so you could wear my elephant sweater." This elephant sweater, which Mama had acquired as a freshman, was not as funny as it sounded. Knit of creamy wool and designed in homage to the University of Alabama mascot, it featured a parade of little red elephants marching across the bosom. Though this sweater had undoubtedly made an indelible impression on Mama's fans, I realized when I tried it on that it was never going to fit me.

Amy Cole, a tiny blonde who sat next to me in choir, was also excited about going to Tuscaloosa. We had become friends in seventh grade when Amy passed me a note saying "Beer tastes sick, incorporated." Now, Amy's eyes lit up. "We can visit Tori!" she said. Amy's sister Tori was actually named Jean. She was a student at the university and rumored to be living with her boyfriend, Leo, who was actually named Bob. Amy saw this trip as a golden opportunity to confirm the reports, after which she planned to tattle to her parents. She waved her hand. "Miss Bowen! When we go to Tuscaloosa can Kathie and me stay with my sister? She's married," added Amy cannily.

Miss Bowen waved a hand distractedly. "Get a note," she said. I gave Miss Bowen a sympathetic look; she was probably feeling underappreciated. A cloud lingered over her. One day in early spring, in order to "acknowledge the role of popular music," she had put Martha Reeves and the Vandellas on the record player. In response, the school's entire flock of maids had emerged from the woodwork and began dancing down the hall with the janitor. I didn't see how this was Miss Bowen's fault.

I liked Miss Bowen. Cloverdale's only unmarried teacher under the age of sixty, she wore her hair long, like Mia Farrow. Once Miss Bowen caught Deb Hamrick giving someone a test in class. The "test" was just a paper with a squiggly line drawn across it. You were supposed to take a piece of thread and try to put it so it covered the entire wiggly line; whatever you said as you struggled was what you'd say on your wedding night. Miss Bowen not only didn't yell at Deb, she took the test herself and made the winning remark, which was "I can't get this thing to work," though I came in a close second with "whose stupid idea was this?" Miss Bowen was, in fact, probably going to get married in June to somebody named Fred, though she wasn't going to give up her career. "Even if I do get married," she said reassuringly, "I'll still be your teacher next fall."

Both Mama and Mrs. Cole agreed that Amy and I could stay with Tori, and one Friday afternoon we happily boarded the bus for Tuscaloosa. The highway was fairly boring; we sang "99 Bottles of Beer on the Wall," but we faltered after the first dozen or so bottles.

Then, after a lengthy consultation with Deb Hamrick, who was sitting behind her, Amy handed me a small book. It was entitled *Love without Fear* and had a valentine on the cover. I flipped cautiously through it. *Love without Fear* turned out to be a marriage manual. It ran heavily to diagrams, some of which may have been printed upside down, since they didn't look plausible. "Right," I said, handing it back. I wondered if Miss Bowen was having to study this sort of thing.

Rather than looking at books with ridiculous diagrams, I thought we should be practicing for the competition. We were singing a choral version of "Recessional," a poem by Rudyard Kipling. This was a very classy song. It was somber, in contrast to the peppy numbers that the other schools in the regional competition had sung. It was also historical; writing right after Queen Victoria's Diamond Jubilee, Kipling expressed concern about the wars England was waging all across the globe. The poem starts out "God of our fathers, known of old, Lord of our far-flung battle-line" and goes on through a number of sober verses before concluding with "Judge of the nations, spare us yet, Lest we forget, lest we forget." Sung ending in a minor key, the number had clearly wowed the judges, though not everyone was a fan. The old battle-ax choral director from Queen of Sorrows had sneered that it was "very brave to pick such a controversial subject." I assumed she was annoyed that her bunch hadn't won with their rendition of "My Favorite Things." Miss Bowen had just blinked at her.

Eventually, the bus rolled into Tuscaloosa, and Tori met us. A tall brunette, she looked like Olive Oyl, though she was stylishly dressed in a very short skirt and boots with fringe. She stuffed us and our luggage into a Volkswagen Beetle with decals of daisies across the front. "Where'd you get the flowers?" asked Amy. "Leo did them," said Tori proudly. Amy elbowed me. Tori, and probably Leo, lived in an old building called the Casablanca Apartments. The hallway was pitch black, but the apartment was sunny and roomy, with an old-fashioned kitchen and a couch that made out into a bed. There were posters on all the walls; one of them said "Janis Joplin at the Fillmore" in wiggly letters. There were a couple of beanbag chairs and a coffee table covered in wax from a huge striped candle.

Tori left to pick up Leo from work. "Because he's having supper with us," she added hastily, saying that she would be right back and that we should not open the door for any reason. This was a little worrying, as was the headline in the local newspaper which I found under the coffee table. "Campus: Unrest Feared," I read. Apparently the university president was considering ending the semester early due to what the paper referred to as "peaceniks and agitators."

While I read, Amy began searching for evidence that Tori was living with Leo. She didn't find anything incriminating in the bathroom, so she moved on to the closet.

"Look," said Amy. "Birth control pills." She handed me something that looked like a compact. "Where'd you get this?" I asked. "Tori's raincoat pocket," said Amy smugly. I thought we should give Tori the benefit of the doubt. "Well, some people take those things for acne."

"Yeah," said Amy. "Sure."

It turned out that there was more evidence. Amy yanked open the closet: "Look." I looked. There, way in the back, was a big overcoat and boots that obviously belonged to Leo.

Though the case was pretty well closed, I still didn't think we ought to tell, especially since Leo, a tall awkward guy whose long hair was thinning on top, paid for all our dinners at the coffee house. This coffee house was the most unusual diner I'd ever seen. The sign over the door spelled "Coffee" as "Coughie," and the walls were painted black and covered with posters saying "Protest the Draft." "Is there unrest on campus?" I asked worriedly. Tori and Leo burst out laughing.

"Nah," said Leo. "There were some big demonstrations in New York last month, and now everybody's paranoid." Just then our spaghetti arrived, so I dropped the subject. On the way back, we passed the Supply Store steps, which held groups of students sitting, or lying, around. A banner with a peace symbol was strung up over the door. Under it, a guy sat playing a guitar. I wondered if he was a peacenik.

Amy and I slept on the foldout couch, though Amy tried to stay up long enough to see if Leo would really leave.

At breakfast, Leo was nowhere in sight, and Tori had made waffles. "Where'd you get a waffle iron?" asked Amy. "It's Mom's," said Tori. "I found it under the sink. I got her blender, too. Next time y'all come up we'll have strawberry daiquiris."

"Great," said Amy. I nodded. "Are you coming home for the summer?" added Amy. Tori thought. "Nah, I don't guess so," she said. "But y'all could come up on the bus. You can go swimming at the university pool, and we'll go to the free movies on the quad."

"Okay," we both said. Already summer was shaping up better than expected, though I was a little worried—if Amy decided to tell on Tori it would be the end of these summer plans, and probably of Tori's college career. I didn't have time to worry long, though, because we had to change into our blue skirts and blouses for the competition.

On the way to campus, we passed a lot more posters saying "Rally against the Draft" and a couple calling for legalizing marijuana. People were still sitting and lying around on the steps, but my mood stayed light, because our choir was in good voice. We sailed mournfully through "Recessional" with nary a sour note. The audience applauded enthusiastically. I thought we had it in the bag, even though the judges, all of whom were more than one hundred years old, just sat there looking constipated.

We got honorable mention. First place went to Bessemer Junior High for their medley from *Mary Poppins.* We were all annoyed, but Miss Bowen was livid. She headed for the judges' table. After a few minutes of waving her arms, she marched right past us, headed for the pay phone in the hall. She was talking pretty loud; we could hear without being too obvious.

"Thought it was about Viet Nam," she was saying indignantly. She listened a moment, then said, "I guess because they're morons." She apparently figured out we were listening, because she put her hand around the mouthpiece, but I heard her say, ". . . minute we get married I'm quitting."

Everybody was pretty quiet on the bus going home. "Are you going to tell your parents on Tori?" I asked. Amy mulled it over. She may have been thinking about the strawberry daiquiris. "Nah," she said.

PANAMA CITY

Ashwander's Cottages had been torn down, replaced by a Holiday Inn. This was a revolting development. Gulf Shores wouldn't be the same if we had to stay in a Holiday Inn. About the time I heard about Ashwander's, Patty Harris invited me to go to Panama City with her and Annette. It was tempting. The only problem was Patty's mother, Clara.

Clara Harris was popularly assumed to be crazy. Some of it had rubbed off on Patty, but it was hard to see how Patty could have turned out otherwise. For one thing, the Harrises hoarded food. If you made the mistake of eating supper at Patty's, Clara would tell you the age of everything you ate: "Those hot dogs have been in the freezer since 1957."

Patty could be pretty annoying, but Clara's reaction to her was almost literally overkill. A couple of times, she had gone after Patty with a hammer, and, just few weeks before the beach invitation, Clara had tried to run over Patty in the parking lot at Sears.

I often wondered why nobody bothered to call the police on Clara. In fact, I urged Patty to do so, but she said Clara's rejoinder was that if Patty called the police on her, she would call the police on Patty for failure to clean her room. This struck me as a weak argument.

Annette and I weren't scared to go places with Clara, though, since she wasn't going to belt anybody who looked like a believable witness. This was how she had kept her job teaching tough slum kids.

Annette was five months older than I was, and a year older than Patty. Since her family went to the same Catholic church as Patty's, she got dragooned into spending time with her. Occasionally, hanging around with Patty and Annette paid off; this beach invitation was just the latest example.

On a hot July morning, I piled into the backseat of Clara's car, which already held Annette, Annette's huge grocery sack, and Annette's hair dryer. As we pulled out of town, "Last Train to Clarksville" came on the radio. Patty turned it up. Clara turned it off. Patty looked glum; Annette and I were relieved, since we considered the Monkees lame, partly because Patty had announced she had a crush on Davy Jones. Clara turned the radio dial to a station that played elevator music. Mantovani flowed from the dashboard; Annette rolled her eyes.

Panama City had a number of extremely glamorous motels, one of which featured purple spotlights. Unfortunately, we pulled into a mom-and-pop motel called Porter's Court. Annette referred to it as Porter's Pot. Patty and I immediately ran down to the beach. I was relieved to see that the Gulf and the white dunes were exactly the same as at Gulf Shores. Annette, who was worried about her hair, stayed by the pool.

When we got back to the room, we were surprised to find it was cold. In fact, it was freezing. "What's wrong with this air-conditioner?" I asked, fiddling with the knobs.

"Leave that!" snapped Clara. She was wearing an orange outfit with pants that looked like bloomers. She resembled something you'd see at Halloween. "It's at sixty-two degrees. That's what the Fedders Corporation says is the ideal interior temperature."

I thought that the Fedders Corporation should mind its own business. "They're the ones that made our air-conditioner," said Patty complacently. Annette put her enormous bag of food in the refrigerator. She could have just put it on the air-conditioner.

When we finished changing into our unimaginative one-piece swimsuits, we went over to the pool. We'd each brought a beach towel. Mine showed a person muffled up in a long-sleeve muumuu and hat.

The caption read "To Heck with a Tan." Patty's showed a person in water up to their eyes. The caption read "Keep Your Head above the Water." Annette's showed a penguin. The caption read "Cool for Sure." Annette, who had obviously won the towel contest, unwrapped her lunch. She always brought her own food. Today she had pickled eggplant sandwiches made by her mother. It was pretty loud by the pool, since the Porters had rigged up a sound system, which was now blasting a polka. "Foot-stompin' music," said Annette.

Luckily, Annette had brought a transistor radio which she turned up full blast. "Summer in the City" magically started playing. When the news came on, Annette switched it off in favor of a song that she had learned from one of her hundreds of cousins. To the tune of "Bridge on the River Kwai," she sang, "Comet, it makes your teeth turn green, Comet, it tastes like gasoline, Comet will make you vomit, So get your Comet and vomit todayyyyy." Patty was overjoyed. I could imagine her belting out "Comet" at school, only to be killed by a passing nun.

It was getting hot; I fanned myself with my *Seventeen*. Annette announced casually that she was really nervous about starting high school in the fall. This "high school" business was a mere technicality. Catholic High started in ninth grade, unlike Lanier where I would go in fall 1967, if I lived that long. Patty then weighed in smugly, "I'm going to Jeff Davis. Mother said so." Jeff Davis was the new public high school. Rumor had it that it was built solely so that snob kids wouldn't have to go to Lanier.

Patty's announcement was par for the course. If somebody bragged about something, Clara would mastermind Patty's effort to one-up them. Take the tape recorder. For Christmas, I had gotten a cassette tape recorder. Clara had promptly gone out and gotten Patty a four-hundred-dollar reel-to-reel model. Probably the Monkees were saving up to get one just like it.

Meanwhile, there was no getting around the fact that I didn't go to Catholic school, which meant I didn't have to wear a uniform. "Look at this," I said, waving *Seventeen* under Annette and Patty's collective nose. The full-page ad, which was captioned "Thigh-High for Fall," showed a model in an extremely short skirt. Annette and Patty glared.

Mama had given me some money and told me to treat Patty to a nice meal, so we walked next door to the Dixie Hot Shop where Patty and I ate seventy-nine-cent hamburgers and Annette drank a Tab. The Hot Shop's radio was playing "Paperback Writer." I shook my head. The Beatles must have gone insane. Who wanted to listen to a song about some jerk wanting to write books?

That afternoon, we went for a long walk on the beach, and I got sunburned. I retreated to the room, which was still glacial, and read my magazine while Annette and Patty continued to grill themselves.

For supper, Clara produced some mummified hot dogs that had been in her freezer since election night, 1960. Annette was having another eggplant sandwich. "Got any more of that eggplant?" I asked, edging away from the hot dogs. It tuned out Annette had brought a couple of gallons of pickled eggplant, so I dug in. That night, I was so cold I couldn't sleep. I finally found a blanket that some winter guest of the Porters had left in the closet.

The next morning, Patty and I had Cocoa Puffs for breakfast, and Annette had her usual, a tuna sandwich and a Coke. She insisted on toasting the bread in the kitchenette's tiny oven, explaining that toast had fewer calories than bread. Annette was a fount of useful information.

I was still sunburned. I put vinegar on my arms, which made me smell like a salad. I spent most of the day sitting in the shade, listening to Mom and Pop Porter's polkas. At least we didn't see much of Clara, who was haranguing the Porters about Vatican II. Then Patty pulled a coup by getting Clara to agree to take us to the Miracle Strip Amusement Park. This would have been ideal if Clara hadn't insisted we eat in the room first to save money. Clara had some war-surplus yogurt, Patty had another antique hot dog, and Annette and I had eggplant.

The biggest attraction at the Miracle Strip was the Tornado roller coaster. The ride's loudspeaker blared "Telstar," but you couldn't hear much over the screaming. We rode the roller coaster three times, after which Patty threw up. Clara yelled at her for a couple of minutes, but people were starting to stare at her so she shut up and dragged us all to the car. I felt rather gloomy on the ride back, even though Clara had subsided. We were headed for another freezing night. That's when I saw it, looming over us. "Look!" I yelled. An enormous full-color billboard featured a woman relaxing on a couch next to a large window-unit air-conditioner. The caption, in big red letters, was "Keep your home at a comfortable 69 degrees all summer with Fedders!"

"See?" I demanded. "Sixty-nine degrees."

"That must be the latest model," added Annette slyly.

Clara knew when she was beaten. Seven degrees wasn't that much warmer, but at least it was survivable. That night I sprayed myself with Solarcaine and slept soundly.

The next morning, back at the pool, I took stock. We were all still alive; we weren't freezing; and, thanks to Annette, there was plenty to eat, provided you liked eggplant.

There were probably easier ways to get to the beach, and eventually I would think of one.

Meanwhile, the Gulf glimmered in the sun, there was a nice breeze blowing, and Annette's transistor radio was blasting the Cyrkle's only hit: "I think it's gonna be all right. Yes, the worst is over now. The morning sun is shining like a red rubber ball."

SICK ROOM

So far, ninth grade was not living up to my expectations, although they had been low. For one thing, my plans to upgrade my wardrobe had come to naught. Mama had given me some money to buy an outfit, then had gotten annoyed when I spent fifteen dollars on a skirt that admittedly did look a lot like burlap. I was not the only one in Mrs. Sweatt's homeroom with wardrobe problems, though; the first day of class a mean fat girl named Cheryl Sanders had shown up in an orange tent dress and had been referred to as the Great Pumpkin ever since. Mrs. Sweatt, a hard-bitten old woman who looked as if she wrestled alligators in her spare time, was supposed to be teaching us Latin. This would have been bad enough without her habit of suddenly lecturing us on things she didn't like. "French gals," she intoned one fall morning, "is common. They show they navels in them bikinis." As she spoke, she glared at Pam Raney, probably suspecting her of harboring a bikini.

Pam had white hair. She hadn't suffered a fright or anything; she had just gotten carried away while trying to become a platinum blonde. She also wore white lipstick, short skirts, and a lot of blue eye shadow. She looked kind of like Twiggy, but I didn't mention it for fear she would take offense and beat me senseless.

I knew all about Pam Raney beating people senseless, because a couple of days earlier I had accidentally sat at the wrong lunch table. This table was the official headquarters of Blair Kellett and Joanie Jerrold. While not exactly popular, they had found a niche as the ninth grade's most feared social critics. When I plunked myself down, they scowled at me. This was all the more impressive since they could have passed for twins. Same Bobbie Brooks shirtwaist dresses, same Bass Weejuns, same dishwater-blonde hair worn in the same bubble cut. Joanie Jerrold's mouthful of braces somewhat spoiled the effect, but she mostly let Blair do the talking. I shrugged, indicating that there were no seats at other tables and that they were going to have to take it or leave it. Whatever insulting remarks they were planning on passing went unsaid, because at that moment Pam Raney, laughing raucously, knocked over a chair. The two critics smirked identically, and Blair hauled out a spiral notebook. This was their Slam Book. The Slam Book had been invented by somebody who got tired of just writing stuff about people on the blackboard. Properly maintained, the Slam Book provided a valuable archive of nasty remarks and was capable of being updated in case you had overlooked something. I was concentrating on eating my pimiento cheese, but I unobtrusively glanced up in time to see Blair record something in her book, after which she muttered, "That's the last page. I'll have to bring another one tomorrow." When she and Joanie trundled up to the front to deposit their trays, they left the book in plain sight. I grabbed it, studiously avoided the "F" section, since I didn't want to know, and flipped right to the back. "PAM RAINY," I read. Spelling was not Blair's strong suit. "Juvenal delinquint. Beat a girl senseles." That was the last entry. On the back cover of the notebook Blair had written "SO ENDETH ANOTHER SLAMETH BOOK."

Slameth. "Not bad," I thought, hastily replacing the book.

Since that incident, I had kept a wary eye on Pam Raney. She was a loud, argumentative girl and I could see her beating people senseless. She didn't hang around with anyone except Cristle Giddens. I wasn't sure if Cristle's family had been trying to name her Crystal. If

I'd had time I could have looked her up in the Slam Book, although there was a good chance that Blair spelled "Crystal" the same way. Cristle was a big, meaty, mean-looking brunette who wore homemade dresses and sneakers, in contrast to Pam Raney who dressed like a French gal. I made it my business to stay out of their way.

Mrs. Sweatt finished her rundown on various groups of people who were, she said, the scum of the earth and finally gave us some actual Latin. She had already pointed out that since Latin was a dead language no one really knew how the words were supposed to be pronounced. Just as well, I thought, listening to her quote Julius Caesar. "Wienie Weedy Weeki!" she brayed.

I felt increasingly certain that I was overdue for an afternoon in the Sick Room.

The Sick Room didn't look like much. It had a window and a sofa bed for people who were sick and was about the size of a large closet. It was at one end of Cloverdale School; from the window it was possible to watch your unlucky classmates headed for the cafeteria. It was also possible to slide out the back door, though sometimes a teacher would suddenly appear in the doorway to make sure you hadn't escaped.

Claiming to be sick at Cloverdale School involved whole layers of bureaucracy. If you wanted to leave school, you had to telephone one of your parents, who had to speak to the principal's secretary, Mrs. Tipton. But if all you wanted was to go to the Sick Room, it was sufficient to pretend to phone someone, ask piteously to be allowed to leave school, pretend to listen, and then ask, "Well, can I at least go to the Sick Room?"

Mrs. Tipton was probably under the impression that spending the afternoon in the Sick Room was not an attractive alternative to spending the afternoon in class. In reality, visiting the Sick Room was sort of like a trip to your own private reading room. Right now, I was settled back on the sofa bed, reading a book of familiar quotations; it was the only book I had small enough to fit in my purse. As usual, I had the Sick Room to myself. "The voice of the People is the voice of God," I read. This was a depressing thought. The author was some Roman I'd never heard of. I was reminded of Latin class; another depressing thought.

I was just considering Edmund Burke's remark, "Early and provident fear is the mother of safety," when the door flew open and Pam and Cristle barreled in, laughing. Pam was brandishing a Coke.

I instantly vacated the sofa bed and perched nervously on a folding chair in the corner. I would probably have just run out of the room, had I not been paralyzed with horror. Pam and Cristle flopped down on the sofa bed.

Pam looked right at me. "I don't guess you got any gum, do you?" she asked.

"Uh, no," I admitted. This didn't seem to surprise either of them. I reburied myself in my book, in which somebody named Thomas Fuller was quoted as saying "It is cruel to beat a cripple with his own crutches." I fervently agreed.

Suddenly I became aware that the conversation between Pam and Cristle had taken a serious turn. "Stepfather," Cristle was saying, followed by something I couldn't hear, followed by "asshole."

Pam in turn said something I couldn't hear, followed in a somewhat louder voice with "jail." I hesitantly glanced up. Cristle was staring at the floor. Pam was staring at Cristle.

My book had moved on to George Bernard Shaw: "If parents would only realize how they bore their children!"

Cristle stood up and brushed off her unattractive homemade skirt. "I'm going," she said.

"I thought you didn't want to go home," said Pam. Cristle shook her head. "I'm going to Bob Nuckels's."

This was a surprise. I hastily looked back down at my book. Bob Nuckels was a shadowy figure who had opened up a slot-car racetrack in an empty storefront a couple of blocks from the school. I had been once with Ray and Clay. The crowd consisted mostly of little boys, absently watching the slot cars go round and round. There was a back room, but people seemed to avoid it. Right after that visit, Ray and Clay had announced that they were never going back to Bob Nuckels's, because Bob Nuckels was a pervert. My mother had made some attempt to investigate, but the men she talked to at the grocery store next to Speedy Slots were indignant, saying that Bob Nuckels was "the only person who had ever tried to do anything for these kids." I had pointed out that the day I went to Bob

Nuckels's, I had noticed that he bought Cokes by the caseload from this grocery. "I don't know what to think," Mama had said. Ray and Clay, who apparently knew what to think, never went back there. Now I figured that Cristle was either brave or really stupid, or else Bob Nuckels was such a complete pervert that he didn't even bother with girls.

Cristle waddled out. Peace reigned.

I glanced through a selection of quotes from William Faulkner: "The past is never dead. It's not even past." Then I felt someone looking at me.

"Hey," said Pam. I glanced around to see who she was talking to, but there wasn't anybody else in the corner. "Yeah, you," elaborated Pam. "Have you got a father?"

Well, I hadn't. "Uh, no," I said, wondering if this was some sort of conversational gambit that would end with me getting beaten senseless.

Pam smiled. "Me neither," she said. In a voice gentler than any I'd ever heard from her, she added, "It just makes it easier, doesn't it?"

I thought this over for two or three seconds. Then I nodded. Pam rooted through her fringed purse and pulled out a transistor radio. "Devil in a Blue Dress" filled the room.

We listened in companionable silence. I read a quote from Robert Browning: "Every joy is gain. And gain is gain, however small."

1967

"Hi, my name's Lizzie Holt and I'm lost. Where's the art room?" I eyed the blonde fat girl with deep suspicion. In the first place, this was January. Anybody would know where the art room was by this time. In the second place, this was Cloverdale School. Telling a stranger you needed help was about like walking up to a lion and saying "Hi! I'm a wounded wildebeest."

On the off chance that this wasn't some sort of *Candid Camera* thing, I pointed. "I'm Kathie Farnell, and it's over there." I was, unfortunately, headed that way myself.

The art room, which sounded like it would be a good place, was a disreputable hovel huddled at the edge of the school barbecue pit. By the time we reached the door, I had found out that Lizzie Holt was an air force kid, which was why she was just showing up at Cloverdale after the year was half over. Her father, who was actually from Montgomery, would be retiring here; her family lived in Jasmine Hills. This was big news. Jasmine Hills was tucked away in the woods near Wetumpka. The area had been the site of fabulous gardens created by a millionaire—someone so staggeringly wealthy that he allowed the general public to roam, free of charge, through his estate. I had spent many a relaxing Sunday afternoon feeding the Jasmine Hills goldfish. And Lizzie lived within walking distance of this magical place, which was almost like living within walking distance of the Eiffel Tower.

We had now reached the door of the art room, which was open in spite of the cold. "Well, here it—DUCK!!"

Lizzie ducked, avoiding a fusillade of chalk. Apparently Bobby Duggar, one of the dumbest-looking guys in the class, had been smart enough to figure out that if you dump a large box of broken chalk into an oscillating fan, something is bound to happen.

We shoved our way into the room. As usual, Mrs. Warner, the teacher, wasn't there. This showed common sense on her part, since the classroom scene this morning included twenty or thirty kids throwing paint, climbing on top of the cabinets, and hitting each other with folding chairs.

Eventually, the back door of the room opened and Mrs. Warner, hiccuping gently, weaved in. She collapsed into her chair, favored us with a bleary smile, and went to sleep.

"Is it always like this?" asked Lizzie.

"Nah," I said. "Things are pretty quiet today because of the cold."

Possibly it was because her family was actually from Montgomery, but Lizzie was nowhere near as weird and obnoxious as the average air force kid. I had met one girl who was keeping a scrapbook of murders that had happened every place she lived. Then there was the appalling family who lived in the next block. Once one of their numerous children announced smugly that they ate boysenberry jam at breakfast every day. I understood him to say "poison berry." That explains a lot, I thought.

The first time I spent the night at Lizzie's, we had spaghetti. I had eaten spaghetti once at Annette's. Her family ate a lot of odd things, like pickled eggplant and fried green beans, so I hadn't been surprised. It was sort of a shock, though, to see it at Lizzie's. When we arrived at Lizzie's house, her mother, a big solid blonde, had been in the kitchen buttering a whole loaf of garlic bread. I watched, fascinated. Lizzie's father, also big and solid but redheaded, had said "Hello, girls" as we passed through the den, but then went back to reading the *Alabama Journal*. I was enthused that we were having spaghetti, but as soon as we sat down Lizzie's sister Jane overturned a glass of water. It wasn't a full glass, but still. Before I could stop myself I had ducked down in my chair, protecting my head with both arms.

Then, nothing happened.

"Oh, Jane, honestly," said Lizzie. "Jane, be more careful," said Lizzie's father. "Really, Jane," said Lizzie's mother.

"I didn't mean to," whined Jane. I cautiously opened one eye, then the other. Fortunately everyone was still shifting around trying to avoid the water and telling Jane to get a mop, so I was able to crawl out from under the table, pretending I had just dropped my napkin.

After supper, Lizzie and I went upstairs. "Look at this," Lizzie said, opening a door. I stared. The room was completely black, even the ceiling. A bead curtain hung over the closet door. The bed had an Indian spread, and painted on one wall was a huge peace sign that glowed in the dark. This room belonged to Lizzie's older sister Anne, who was at school in Washington. "Anne got arrested," Lizzie reported proudly. "Wow! What'd she do?" Lizzie eyed me severely. "Nothing. She was in a peace demonstration. They arrested everybody there. Daddy was really mad. He had to call our uncle in Washington to get her out."

Lizzie's room was fairly tame by comparison. She had a desk under the window with a view of the woods and a shelf full of books she'd gotten in Germany with titles in ominous Gothic lettering. On one wall was a poster, a woodcut of a famished-looking guy raising his hands and saying something in Russian. "What's he saying?" I asked. Lizzie shrugged, "'Help,' I guess."

When I got home I announced that I wanted to paint the room I was now sharing with Mama.

"Purple," I said.

"Purple?" said Mama.

"Lilac," I said.

The paint color that Mama picked out—"April in Paris"—was pretty, especially with the white Cape Cod curtains she also picked out, but the effect wasn't exactly what I had in mind. I didn't even bother getting a peace sign, much less a poster of a Russian saying "Help." I decided just to tell people I had a purple room without going into the details.

There was no reason, though, not to upgrade our meals.

"Can we have spaghetti?" I asked Mama. Mama considered. "If you can figure out how to make it." I looked up "spaghetti" in the international section of the World War II–era cookbook that Mama had gotten for a wedding present. I could tell this was going to be tricky because the recipe called for garlic and a colander, neither of which we had. At least I hadn't wanted Chinese food. Where would we have gotten a wok?

The spaghetti, which I made with garlic powder, was a big hit. I had to strain it the way we strained everything, by sticking a fork in the hole left by the missing knob of the pot lid, then maneuvering the pot over the sink. At this point I discovered that if spaghetti falls in the sink, the best thing is to pretend it didn't.

I went back to Lizzie's as often as possible. The second time I visited, we had spaghetti again. "Oh Mom!" said Lizzie. "We just had spaghetti!" She seemed embarrassed. "It's okay," I said. "This is really great." I suspected Lizzie's mother had gotten actual garlic from somewhere.

We read fashion magazines together but Lizzie was doubtful that she could carry off the latest looks, since she was in fact a tall, fat blonde with a pageboy haircut. I looked a lot more like Twiggy than she did, except for the hair. I tried to console her by pointing to a photo of Mama Cass, but it didn't work.

In addition to fashion magazines, Lizzie had a book called *Little Known Facts* which included all sorts of weird sidelights from history. One of my favorite items was about the Republic of Venice and the legend that it was founded by a tribe of people who had fled into the marshes to escape hordes of bloodthirsty savages. When they reached the marshes, they felt pretty confident that they could survive, so they named their new home "Venezia," which roughly translated to "We made it this far." If we weren't reading something, Lizzie and I listened to her albums, which included *Sounds of Silence* and *The Peter Paul and Mary Album*. Inspired, I got those same albums and played them on our old hi-fi. I also decided to ask for a record player for my birthday, since the record player I'd gotten in 1960 only played 45s. Once I even got to meet Lizzie's sister Anne, a big sad girl with her hair in a braid. She was home recuperating from having come down with scurvy as a result of her macrobiotic diet. Lizzie reported that her father was making Anne transfer to Auburn. "He was really irate," she said. I wondered how she could tell, since I had never seen her father hit people, throw things, or even scream.

The night before ninth-grade graduation, Mama took us to Shakey's for pizza. As we waited for the order, Mama updated us on her work situation. Jimmy Cates, the lawyer she worked for, was having problems defending a robber who was, Mama said, guilty as all get-out.

Lizzie looked concerned. "But," she said, "how can you be sure he's guilty?"

"Because," said Mama grimly, "it's written all over him."

At this point the pizza arrived. "This," said Lizzie somewhat indistinctly, "is way better than what I had the other night."

"Where'd you go?" I asked. "Tony's?" I liked Tony's pizza but we never got to go since it was on the Atlanta Highway and, according to Mama, driving on the Atlanta Highway was taking your life in your hands.

Lizzie shook her head. "No, my mom made it. There wasn't nearly enough cheese."

I was amazed. So was Mama. "I don't think I could ever make my own pizza," she said worriedly. "You have to have that yeast."

Mama went to get her tea refilled. I was just musing on what it would be like to have homemade pizza when Lizzie sighed tragically. "I really envy you," she said.

"What??" I said, louder than I had intended.

"Your mom's a lawyer. That must be great. I mean, your mom has a career and all mine ever does is teach Sunday school and drive us around."

"But," I said, bewildered, "she can make spaghetti."

It was the last day of school, and it was hot.

Lizzie Holt and I stood on the front steps waiting to be lined up for graduation. We each had on the obligatory white dresses. Mine had long, flaring lace sleeves. Lizzie's was pretty plain. It had short sleeves, though, so at least it was cool.

I waved at Pam Raney, who waved back. She and I had had several interesting conversations in the Sick Room, though usually we just played cards. It went without saying that it wouldn't do either of us any good socially to be seen in public together. "She looks just like Twiggy," said Lizzie mournfully. It was true. Pam was wearing a dress short enough to pass as a skimpy blouse. I knew I wouldn't be seeing Pam any more. She and Cristle were going to Lee, universally regarded as the redneck high school. The meanest girls were going to the brand-new Jeff Davis, and everybody else, including me and Lizzie, to Lanier. I'd never see most of these people again. This was the most encouraging thought I'd had in weeks.

"That's the way, a nice big smile," said Mama approvingly, motioning everybody on the steps to huddle closer together. She had rented a Polaroid camera. "Smile, everybody. Say 'cheese.'"

"Venezia," I said.